S0-BOG-792

AN AMERICAN IDYLL
THE LIFE OF
CARLETON H. PARKER

Carleton H. Parker

AN AMERICAN IDYLL

THE LIFE OF
CARLETON H. PARKER

By

CORNELIA STRATTON PARKER

BOSTON
THE ATLANTIC MONTHLY PRESS
1919

COPYRIGHT, 1919, BY THE ATLANTIC MONTHLY COMPANY

COPYRIGHT, 1919, BY THE ATLANTIC MONTHLY PRESS

ALL RIGHTS RESERVED

The poem on the opposite page is here reprinted with the express permission of Messrs. Charles Scribner's Sons, publishers of Robert Louis Stevenson's Works.

Yet, O stricken heart, remember, O remember,
How of human days he lived the better part.
April came to bloom, and never dim December
Breathed its killing chill upon the head or heart.

Doomed to know not Winter, only Spring, a being
Trod the flowery April blithely for a while,
Took his fill of music, joy of thought and seeing,
Came and stayed and went, nor ever ceased to smile.

Came and stayed and went, and now when all is finished,
You alone have crossed the melancholy stream,
Yours the pang, but his, O his, the undiminished,
Undecaying gladness, undeparted dream.

All that life contains of torture, toil, and treason,
Shame, dishonor, death, to him were but a name.
Here, a boy, he dwelt through all the singing season
And ere the day of sorrow departed as he came.

Written for our three children.

Dedicated to all those kindred souls, friends of Carl Parker whether they knew him or not, who are making the fight, without bitterness but with all the understanding, patience, and enthusiasm they possess, for a saner, kindlier, and more joyous world.

And to those especially who love greatly along the way.

PREFACE

It was a year ago to-day that Carl Parker died — March 17, 1918. His fortieth birthday would have come on March 31. His friends, his students, were free to pay their tribute to him, both in the press and in letters which I treasure. I alone of all, — I who knew him best and loved him most, — had no way to give some outlet to my soul; could see no chance to pay *my* tribute.

One and another have written of what was and will be his valuable service to economic thought and progress; of the effects of his mediation of labor disputes, in the Northwest and throughout the nation; and of his inestimable qualities as friend, comrade, and teacher.

"He gave as a Federal mediator," — so runs one estimate of him, — "all his unparalleled knowledge and understanding of labor and its point of view. That knowledge, that understanding he gained, not by academic investigation, but by working in mines and woods, in shops and on farms. He had the trust and confidence of both sides in disputes between labor and capital; his services were called in whenever trouble was brewing. . . . Thanks to him, strikes were averted; war-work of the most vital importance, threatened by misunderstandings and smouldering discontent, went on."

But almost every one who has written for publication has told of but one side of him, and there were such countless sides. Would it then be so out of place if I, his wife, could write of all of him, even to the manner of husband he was?

I have hesitated for some months to do this. He had not yet made so truly national a name, perhaps, as to warrant any assumption that such a work would be acceptable. Many of his close friends have asked me to do just this, however; for they realize, as I do so strongly, that his life was so big, so full, so potential, that, even as the story of a man, it would be worth the reading.

And, at the risk of sharing intimacies that should be kept in one's heart only, I long to have the world know something of the life we led together.

An old friend wrote: "Dear, splendid Carl, the very embodiment of life, energized and joyful to a degree I have never known. And the thought of the separation of you two makes me turn cold. . . . The world can never be the same to me with Carl out of it. I loved his high spirit, his helpfulness, his humor, his adoration of you. Knowing you and Carl, and seeing your life together, has been one of the most perfect things in my life."

An Eastern professor, who had visited at our home from time to time wrote: "You have lost one of the finest husbands I have ever known. Ever since I have known the Parker family, I have considered their home life as ideal. I had hoped that the too few hours I spent in your home might be multiplied many times in coming years. . . . I have never known a man more in love with a woman than Carl was with you."

So I write of him for these reasons: because I must, to ease my own pent-up feelings; because his life was so well worth writing about; because so many friends have sent word to me: "Some day, when you have the time, I hope you will sit down and write me about Carl" — the newer friends asking especially about his earlier years, the older friends wishing to know of his later interests,

and especially of the last months, and of — what I have
written to no one as yet — his death. I can answer them
all this way.

And, lastly, there is the most intimate reason of all. I
want our children to know about their father — not just
his academic worth, his public career, but the life he led
from day to day. If I live till they are old enough to understand, I, of course, can tell them. If not, how are they
to know? And so, in the last instance, this is a document
for them.

C. S. P.

March 17, 1919

AN AMERICAN IDYLL

CHAPTER I

SUCH hosts of memories come tumbling in on me.
More than fifteen years ago, on September 3, 1903, I
met Carl Parker. He had just returned to college, two
weeks late for the beginning of his Senior year. There
was much concern among his friends, for he had gone
on a two months' hunting-trip into the wilds of Idaho,
and had planned to return in time for college. I met
him his first afternoon in Berkeley. He was on the top
of a step-ladder, helping put up an awning for our
sorority dance that evening, uttering his proverbial
joyous banter to any one who came along, be it the
man with the cakes, the sedate house-mother, fellow
awning-hangers, or the girls busying about.

Thus he was introduced to me — a Freshman of
two weeks. He called down gayly, "How do you do,
young lady?" Within a week we were fast friends, I
looking up to him as a Freshman would to a Senior,
and a Senior seven years older than herself at that.
Within a month I remember deciding that, if ever I
became engaged, I would tell Carl Parker before I told
any one else on earth!

After about two months, he called one evening with
his pictures of Idaho. Such a treat as my mountain-
loving soul did have! I still have the map he drew
that night, with the trails and camping-places marked.

And I said, innocence itself, "*I'm* going to Idaho on my honeymoon!" And he said, "I'm not going to marry till I find a girl who wants to go to Idaho on her honeymoon!" Then we both laughed.

But the deciding event in his eyes was when we planned our first long walk in the Berkeley hills for a certain Saturday, November 22, and that morning it rained. One of the tenets I was brought up on by my father was that bad weather was *never* an excuse for postponing anything; so I took it for granted that we would start on our walk as planned.

Carl telephoned anon and said, "Of course the walk is off."

"But why?" I asked.

"The rain!" he answered.

"As if that makes any difference!"

At which he gasped a little and said all right, he'd be around in a minute; which he was, in his Idaho outfit, the lunch he had suggested being entirely responsible for bulging one pocket. Off we started in the rain, and such a day as we had! We climbed Grizzly Peak, — only we did not know it for the fog and rain, — and just over the summit, in the shelter of a very drippy oak tree, we sat down for lunch. A fairly sanctified expression came over Carl's face as he drew forth a rather damp and frayed-looking paper-bag — as a king might look who uncovered the chest of his most precious court jewels before a courtier deemed worthy of that honor. And before my puzzled and somewhat doubtful eyes he spread his treasure — jerked bear-meat, nothing but jerked bear-meat. I never had seen jerked anything, let alone tasted it. I was used to the conventional picnic sandwiches done up in waxed paper, plus a stuffed egg, fruit, and cake. I was ready for a lunch after the conservative pattern, and here I gazed upon a mess of most unappetizing-looking, wrinkled, shrunken, jerked bear-meat, the rain dropping down on it through the oak tree.

I would have gasped if I had not caught the look of awe and reverence on Carl's face as he gazed eagerly, and with what respect, on his offering. I merely took a hunk of what was supplied, set my teeth into it, and pulled. It was salty, very; it looked queer, tasted queer, *was* queer. Yet that lunch! We walked farther, sat now and then under other drippy trees, and at last decided that we must slide home, by that time soaked to the skin, and I minus the heel to one shoe.

I had just got myself out of the bath and into dry clothes when the telephone rang. It was Carl. Could he come over to the house and spend the rest of the afternoon? It was then about four-thirty. He came, and from then on things were decidedly — different.

How I should love to go into the details of that Freshman year of mine! I am happier right now writing about it than I have been in six months. I shall not go into detail — only to say that the night of the Junior Prom of my Freshman year Carl Parker asked me to marry him, and two days later, up again in our hills, I said that I would. To think of that now — to think of waiting two whole days to decide whether I would marry Carl Parker or not!! And for fourteen years from the day I met him, there was never one small moment of misunderstanding, one day that was not happiness — except when we were parted. Perhaps there are people who would consider it stupid, boresome, to live in such peace as that. All I can answer is that it was *not* stupid, it was *not* boresome — oh, how far from it! In fact, in those early days we took our vow that the one thing we would never do was to let the world get commonplace for us; that the time should never come when we would not be eager for the start of each new day. The Kipling poem we loved the most, for it was the spirit of both of us, was "The Long Trail." You know the last of it: —

> The Lord knows what we may find, dear lass,
> And the Deuce knows what we may do —
> But we're back once more on the old trail, our
> own trail, the out trail,
> We're down, hull down, on the Long Trail — the
> trail that is always new!

CHAPTER II

AFTER we decided to get married, and that as soon as ever we could,—I being a Freshman at the ripe and mature age of, as mentioned, just eighteen years, he a Senior, with no particular prospects, not even sure as yet what field he would go into, — we began discussing what we might do and where we might go. Our main idea was to get as far away from everybody as we could, and live the very fullest life we could, and at last we decided on Persia. Why Persia? I cannot recall the steps now that brought us to that conclusion. But I know that first Christmas I sent Carl my picture in a frilled high-school graduation frock and a silk Persian flag tucked behind it, and that flag remained always the symbol for us that we would never let our lives get stale, never lose the love of adventure, never "settle down," intellectually at any rate.

Can you see my father's face that sunny March day, — Charter Day it was, — when we told him we were engaged? (My father being the conventional, traditional sort who had never let me have a real "caller" even, lest I become interested in boys and think of matrimony too young!) Carl Parker was the first male person who was ever allowed at my home in the evening. He came seldom, since I was living in Berkeley most of the time, and anyway, we much preferred prowling all over our end of creation, servant-girl-and-policeman fashion. Also, when I married, according to father it was to be some one, preferably an attorney of parts, about to become a judge, with a large bank account. Instead, at eighteen, I and this almost-unknown-to-him Senior stood before him and said, "We are going to be married," or words to that general effect. And — here is where I want you to think of the expression on my conservative father's face.

Fairly early in the conversation he found breath to say, "And what, may I ask, are your prospects?"

"None, just at present."

"And where, may I ask, are you planning to begin this married career you seem to contemplate?"

"In Persia."

Can you see my father? *"Persia?"*

"Yes, Persia."

"And what, for goodness' sake, are you two going to do in *Persia?"*

"We don't know just yet, of course, but we'll find something."

I can see my father's point of view now, though I am not sure but that I shall prefer a son-in-law for our daughter who would contemplate absolute uncertainty in Persia in preference to an assured legal profession in Oakland, California. It was two years before my father became at all sympathetic, and that condition was far from enthusiastic. So it was a great joy to me to have him say, a few months before his death, "You know, Cornelia, I want you to understand that if I had had the world to pick from I'd have chosen Carl Parker for your husband. Your marriage is a constant source of satisfaction to me."

I saw Carl Parker lose his temper once, and once only. It was that first year that we knew each other. Because there was such a difference between his age and mine, the girls in my sorority house refused to believe there could be anything serious about our going together so much, and took great pains to assure me in private that of course Carl meant nothing by his attentions, — to which I agreed volubly, — and they scolded him in private because it would spoil a Freshman to have a Senior so attentive. We always compared notes later, and were much amused.

But words were one thing, actions another. Since there could be nothing serious in our relationship, naturally there was no reason why we should be left alone. If there was to be a rally or a concert, the Senior sitting at the head of the dinner-table would ask, "How many are going to-night with a man?" Hands. "How many of the girls are going together?" Hands. Then, to me, "Are you going with Carl?" A faint "Yes." "Then we'll all go along with you." Carl stood it twice — twice he beheld this cavalcade bear away in our wake; then he gritted his teeth and announced, "Never again!"

The next college occasion was a rally at the Greek Theatre. Again it was announced at the table that all the unescorted ones would accompany Carl and me. I foresaw trouble. When I came downstairs later, with my hat and coat on, there stood Carl, surrounded by about six girls, all hastily buttoning their gloves, his sister, who knew no more of the truth about Carl and me than the others, being one of them. Never had I seen such a look on Carl's face, and I never did again. His feet were spread apart, his jaw was set, and he was glaring. When he saw me he said, "Come on!" and we dashed for the door.

Sister Helen flew after us. "But Carl — the other girls!"

Carl stuck his head around the corner of the front door, called defiantly, "*Damn* the other girls!" banged the door to, and we fled. Never again were we molested.

Carl finished his Senior year, and a full year it was for him. He was editor of the "Pelican," the University funny paper, and of the "University of California Magazine," the most serious publication on the campus outside the technical journals; he made every "honor" organization there was to make (except the Phi Beta Kappa); he and a fellow student wrote the successful Senior Extravaganza; he was a reader in economics, and graduated with honors. And he saw me every single day.

I feel like digressing here a moment, to assail that old principle — which my father, along with countless others, held so strongly — that a fellow who is really worth while ought to know by his Junior year in college just what his life-work is to be. A few with an early developed special aptitude do, but very few. Carl entered college in August, 1896, in Engineering; but after a term found that it had no further appeal for him. "But a fellow ought to stick to a thing, whether he likes it or not!" If one must be dogmatic, then I say, "A fellow should never work at anything he does not like." One of the things in our case which brought such constant criticism from relatives and friends was that we changed around so much. Thank God we did! It took Carl Parker until he was over thirty before he found just the work he loved the most and in which his soul was content — university work. And he was thirty-seven before he found just the phase of economic study that fired him to his full enthusiasm — his loved field of the application of psychology to economics. And some one would have had him stick to engineering because he started in engineering!

He hurt his knee broad-jumping in his Freshman year at college, and finally had to leave, going to Phœnix, Arizona, and then back to the Parker ranch at Vacaville for the better part of a year. The family was away during that time, and Carl ran the place alone. He returned to college in August, 1898, this time taking up mining. After a year's study in mining he wanted the practical side. In the summer of 1899 he worked underground in the Hidden Treasure Mine, Placer county, California. In 1900 he left college again, going to the gold and copper mines of Rossland, British Columbia. From August, 1900, to May, 1901, he worked in four different mines. It was with considerable feeling of pride that he always added, "I got to be machine man before I quit."

It was at that time that he became a member of the Western Federation of Miners — an historical fact which inimical capitalists later endeavored to make use of from time to time to do him harm. How I loved to listen by the hour to the stories of those grilling days — up at four in the pitch-dark and snow, to crawl to his job, with the blessing of a dear old Scotch landlady and a "pastie"! He would tell our sons of tamping in the sticks of dynamite, till their eyes bulged. The hundreds of times these last six months I've wished I had in writing the stories of those days — of all his days, from early Vacaville times on! Sometimes it would be an old Vacaville crony who would appear, and stories would fly of those boy times — of the exploits up Putah Creek with Pee Wee Allen; of the prayer-meeting when Carl bet he could out-pray the minister's son, and won; of the tediously thought-out assaults upon an ancient hired man on the place, that would fill a book and delight the heart of Tom Sawyer himself; and how his mother used to sigh and add to it all, "If only he had *ever* come home on time to his meals!" (And he has one son just like him. Carl's brothers tell me: "Just give up trying to get Jim home on time. Mamma tried every scheme a human could devise to make Carl prompt for his meals, but nothing ever had the slightest effect. Half an hour past dinner-time he'd still be five miles from home.")

One article that recently appeared in a New York paper began: —

"They say of him that when he was a small boy he displayed the same tendencies that later on made him great in his chosen field. His family possessed a distinct tendency toward conformity and respectability, but Carl was a companion of every 'alley-bum' in Vacaville. His respectable friends never won him

away from his insatiable interest in the under-dog.
They now know it makes valid his claim to achievement."

After the British Columbia mining days, he took
what money he had saved, and left for Idaho, where
he was to meet his chum, Hal Bradley, for his first
Idaho trip — a dream of theirs for years. The Idaho
stories he could tell — oh, why can I not remember
them word for word? I have seen him hold a roomful
of students in Berlin absolutely spellbound over those
adventures — with a bit of Parker coloring, to be
sure, which no one ever objected to. I have seen him
with a group of staid faculty folk sitting breathless at
his Clearwater yarns; and how he loved to tell those
tales! Three and a half months he and Hal were in
— hunting, fishing, jerking meat, trailing after lost
horses, having his dreams of Idaho come true. (If
our sons fail to have those dreams!)

When Hal returned to college, the *Wanderlust* was
still too strong in Carl; so he stopped off in Spokane,
Washington, penniless, to try pot-luck. There were
more tales to delight a gathering. In Spokane he took
a hand at reporting, claiming to be a person of large
experience, since only those of large experience were
desired by the editor of the "Spokesman Review."
He was given sport, society, and the tenderloin to
cover, at nine dollars a week. As he never could go
anywhere without making folks love him, it was not
long before he had his cronies among the "sports,"
kind souls "in society" who took him in, and at least
one strong, loyal friend, — who called him "Bub,"

and gave him much excellent advice that he often used to refer to, — who was the owner of the biggest gambling-joint in town. (Spokane was wide open in those days, and "some town.")

It was the society friends who seem to have saved his life, for nine dollars did not go far, even then. I have heard his hostesses tell of the meal he could consume. "But I'd been saving for it all day, with just ten cents in my pocket." I met a pal of those days who used to save Carl considerable of his nine dollars by "smooching" his wash into his own home laundry.

About then Carl's older brother, Boyd, who was somewhat fastidious, ran into him in Spokane. He tells how Carl insisted he should spend the night at his room instead of going to a hotel.

"Is it far from here?"

"Oh, no!"

So they started out with Boyd's suitcase, and walked and walked through the "darndest part of town you ever saw." Finally, after crossing untold railroad tracks and ducking around sheds and through alleys, they came to a rooming-house that was "a holy fright." "It's all right inside," Carl explained.

When they reached his room, there was one not over-broad bed in the corner, and a red head showing, snoring contentedly.

"Who's that?" the brother asked.

"Oh, a fellow I picked up somewhere."

"Where am I to sleep?"

"Right in here — the bed's plenty big enough for three!"

And Boyd says, though it was 2 A.M. and miles from anywhere, he lit out of there as fast as he could move; and he adds, "I don't believe he even knew that red-headed boy's name!"

The reporting went rather lamely it seemed, however. The editor said that it read amateurish, and he felt he would have to make a change. Carl made for some files where all the daily papers were kept, and read and re-read the yellowest of the yellow. As luck would have it, that very night a big fire broke out in a crowded apartment house. It was not in Carl's "beat," but he decided to cover it anyhow. Along with the firemen, he managed to get up on the roof; he jumped here, he flew there, demolishing the only suit of clothes he owned. But what an account he handed in! The editor discarded entirely the story of the reporter sent to cover the fire, ran in Carl's, word for word, and raised him to twelve dollars a week.

But just as the crown of reportorial success was lighting on his brow, his mother made it plain to him that she preferred to have him return to college. He bought a ticket to Vacaville, — it was just about Christmas time, — purchased a loaf of bread and a can of sardines, and with thirty cents in his pocket, the extent of his worldly wealth, he left for California, traveling in a day coach all the way. I remember his story of how, about the end of the second day of bread and sardines, he cold-bloodedly and with afore-thought cultivated a man opposite him, who looked as if he could afford to eat; and how the man "came through" and asked Carl if he would have dinner with him in the diner. To hear him tell what and how much he ordered, and of the expression and depression of the paying host! It tided him over until he reached home, anyhow — never mind the host.

All his mining experience, plus the dark side of life, as contrasted with society as he saw them both in Spokane, turned his interest to the field of economics. And when he entered college the next spring, it was to "major" in that subject.

May and June, 1903, he worked underground in the coal-mines of Nanaimo. In July he met Nay Moran in Idaho for his second Idaho camping-trip; and it was on his return from this outing that I met him, and ate his jerked meat and loved him, and never stopped doing that for one second.

CHAPTER III

THERE were three boys in the Parker family, and one girl. Each of the other brothers had been encouraged to see the world, and in his turn Carl planned fourteen months in Europe, his serious objective being, on his return, to act as Extension Secretary to Professor Stephens of the University of California, who was preparing to organize Extension work for the first time in California. Carl was to study the English Extension system and also prepare for some Extension lecturing.

By that time, we had come a bit to our senses, and I had realized that since there was no money anyhow to marry on, and since I was so young, I had better stay on and graduate from college. Carl could have his trip to Europe and get an option, perhaps, on a tent in Persia. A friend was telling me recently of running into Carl on the street just before he left for Europe and asking him what he was planning to do for the future. Carl answered with a twinkle, "I don't know but what there's room for an energetic up-and-coming young man in Asia Minor."

I stopped writing here to read through Carl's European letters, and laid aside about seven I wanted to quote from: the accounts of three dinners at Sidney and Beatrice Webb's in London — what knowing them always meant to him! They, perhaps, have forgotten him; but meeting the Webbs and Graham

Wallas and that English group could be nothing but red-letter events to a young economic enthusiast one year out of college, studying Trade-Unionism in the London School of Economics.

Then there was his South-African trip. He was sent there by a London firm, to expert a mine near Johannesburg. Although he cabled five times, said firm sent no money. The bitter disgust and anguish of those weeks — neither of us ever had much patience under such circumstances. But he experted his mine, and found it absolutely worthless; explored the veldt on a second-hand bicycle, cooked little meals of bacon and mush wherever he found himself, and wrote to me. Meanwhile he learned much, studied the coolie question, investigated mine-workings, was entertained by his old college mates—mining experts themselves — in Johannesburg. There was the letter telling of the bull fight at Zanzibar, or Delagoa Bay, or some seafaring port thereabouts, that broke his heart, it was such a disappointment — "it made a Kappa tea look gory by comparison." And the letter that regretfully admitted that perhaps, after all, Persia would not just do to settle down in. About that time he wanted California with a fearful want, and was all done with foreign parts, and declared that any place just big enough for two suited him — it did not need to be as far away as Persia after all. At last he borrowed money to get back to Europe, claiming that "he had learned his lesson and learned it hard." And finally he came home as fast as ever he could reach Berkeley — did not stop even to telegraph.

I had planned for months a dress I knew he would love to have me greet him in. It was hanging ready in the closet. As it was, I had started to retire — in the same room with a Freshman whom I was supposed to be "rushing" hard — when I heard a soft whistle — our whistle — under my window. My heart stopped beating. I just grabbed a raincoat and threw it over me, my hair down in a braid, and in the middle of a sentence to the astounded Freshman I dashed out.

My father had said, "If neither of you changes your mind while Carl is away, I have no objection to your becoming engaged." In about ten minutes after his return we were formally engaged, on a bench up in the Deaf and Dumb Asylum grounds — our favorite trysting-place. It would have been foolish to waste a new dress on that night. I was clad in cloth of gold for all Carl knew or cared, or could see in the dark, for that matter. The deserted Freshman was sound asleep when I got back—and joined another sorority.

Thereafter, for a time, Carl went into University Extension, lecturing on Trade-Unionism and South Africa. It did not please him altogether, and finally my father, a lawyer himself, persuaded him to go into law. Carl Parker in law! How we used to shudder at it afterwards; but it was just one more broadening experience that he got out of life.

Then came the San Francisco earthquake. That was the end of my Junior year, and we felt we had to be married when I finished college — nothing else mattered quite as much as that. So when an offer came out of a clear sky from Halsey and Company, for Carl to be a bond-salesman on a salary that assured matrimony within a year, though in no affluence, and the bottom all out of the law business and no enthusiasm for it anyway, we held a consultation and decided for bonds and marriage. What a bond-salesman Carl made! Those who knew him knew what has been referred to as "the magic of his personality," and could understand how he was having the whole of a small country town asking him to dinner on his second visit.

I somehow got through my Senior year; but how the days dragged! For all I could think of was Carl, Carl, Carl, and getting married. Yet no one — no one on this earth — ever had the fun out of their engaged days that we did, when we were together. Carl used to say that the accumulated expenses of courting me for almost four years came to $10.25. He just guessed at $10.25, though any cheap figure would have done. We just did not care about doing things that happened to cost money. We never did care in our lives, and never would have cared, no matter what our income might be. Undoubtedly that was the main reason we were so blissful on such a small salary in University work — we could never think, at the time, of anything much we were doing without. I remember that the happiest Christmas we almost ever had was over in the country, when we spent under two dollars for all of us. We were absolutely down to bed-rock that year anyway. (It was just after we paid off our European debt.) Carl gave me a book, "The Pastor's Wife," and we gloated over it together all Christmas afternoon! We gave each of the boys a ten-cent cap-pistol and five cents' worth of caps — they were in their Paradise. I mended three shirts of Carl's that had been in my basket so long they were really like new to him, — he'd forgotten he owned them! — laundered them, and hung the trio, tied in tissue paper and red ribbon, on the tree. That *was* a Christmas!

He used to claim, too, that, as I got so excited over five cents' worth of gum-drops, there was no use investing in a dollar's worth of French mixed candy — especially if one had n't the dollar. We always loved tramping more than anything else, and just prowling around the streets arm-in-arm, ending perhaps with an ice-cream soda. Not over-costly, any of it. I have kept some little reminder of almost every spree we took in our four engaged years — it is a book of sheer joy from cover to cover. Except always, always the need of saying good-bye: it got so that it seemed almost impossible to say it.

And then came the day when it did not have to be said each time — that day of days, September 7, 1907, when we were married. Idaho for our honeymoon had to be abandoned, as three weeks was the longest vacation period we could wring from a soulless bond-house. But not even Idaho could have brought us more joy than our seventy-five-mile trip up the Rogue River in Southern Oregon. We hired an old buckboard and two ancient, almost immobile, so-called horses, — they needed scant attention, — and with provisions, gun, rods, and sleeping-bags, we started forth. The woods were in their autumn glory, the fish were biting, corn was ripe along the road-

side, and apples — Rogue River apples — made red
blotches under every tree. "Help yourselves!" the
farmers would sing out, or would not sing out. It was
all one to us.

I found that, along with his every other accomplishment, I had married an expert camp cook. He found
that he had married a person who could not even
boil rice. The first night out on our trip, Carl said,
"You start the rice while I tend to the horses." He
knew I could not cook — I had planned to take a
course in Domestic Science on graduation; however,
he preferred to marry me earlier, inexperienced, than
later, experienced. But evidently he thought even a
low-grade moron could boil rice. The bride of his
heart did not know that rice swelled when it boiled.
We were hungry, we would want lots of rice, so I put
lots in. By the time Carl came back I had partly
cooked rice in every utensil we owned, including the
coffee-pot and the wash-basin. And still he loved me!

That honeymoon! Lazy horses poking unprodded
along an almost deserted mountain road; glimpses of
the river lined with autumn reds and yellows; camp
made toward evening in any spot that looked appealing — and all spots looked appealing; two fish-rods
out; consultation as to flies; leave-taking for half an
hour's parting, while one went up the river to try his
luck, one down. Joyous reunion, with much luck or
little luck, but always enough for supper: trout rolled
in cornmeal and fried, corn on the cob just garnered
from a willing or unwilling farmer that afternoon,
corn-bread, — the most luscious corn-bread in the

world, baked camper-style by the man of the party,
— and red, red apples, eaten by two people who had
waited four years for just that. Evenings in a sandy
nook by the river's edge, watching the stars come out
above the water. Adventures, such as losing Chocolada, the brown seventy-eight-year-old horse, and
finding her up to her neck in a deep stream running
through a grassy meadow with perpendicular banks
on either side. We walked miles till we found a farmer.
With the aid of himself and his tools, plus a stout rope
and a tree, in an afternoon's time we dug and pulled
and hauled and yanked Chocolada up and out onto
dry land, more nearly dead than ever by that time.
The ancient senile had just fallen in while drinking.

We made a permanent camp for one week seventy-
five miles up the river, in a spot so deserted that we
had to cut the road through to reach it. There we
laundered our change of overalls and odds and ends,
using the largest cooking utensil for boiling what was
boiled, and all the food tasted of Ivory soap for two
days; but we did not mind even that. And then, after
three weeks, back to skirts and collars and civilization, and a continued honeymoon from Medford,
Oregon, to Seattle, Washington, doing all the country
banks *en route*. In Portland we had to be separated
for one whole day — it seemed nothing short of
harrowing.

Then came Seattle and house-hunting. We had a
hundred dollars a month to live on, and every apartment we looked at rented for from sixty dollars up.
Finally, in despair, we took two wee rooms, a wee-er

kitchen, and bath, for forty dollars. It was just before
the panic in 1907, and rents were exorbitant. And
from having seventy-five dollars spending money a
month before I was married, I jumped to keeping
two of us on sixty dollars, which was what was left
after the rent was paid. I am not rationalizing when
I say I am glad that we did not have a cent more. It
was a real sporting event to make both ends meet!
And we did it, and saved a dollar or so, just to show
we could. Any and every thing we commandeered to
help maintain our solvency. Seattle was quite given
to food fairs in those days, and we kept a weather
eye out for such. We would eat no lunch, make for the
Food Show about three, nibble at samples all afternoon, and come home well-fed about eight, having
bought enough necessities here and there to keep our
consciences from hurting.

Much of the time Carl had to be on the road selling
bonds, and we almost grieved our hearts out over
that. In fact, we got desperate, and when Carl was
offered an assistant cashiership in a bank in Ellens-
burg, Washington, we were just about to accept it,
when the panic came, and it was all for retrenchment
in banks. Then we planned farming, planned it with
determination. It was too awful, those good-byes.
Each got worse and harder than the last. We had
divine days in between, to be sure, when we'd prowl
out into the woods around the city, with a picnic lunch,
or bummel along the waterfront, ending at a counter
we knew, which produced, or the man behind it produced, delectable and cheap clubhouse sandwiches.

The bond business, and business conditions generally in the Northwest, got worse and worse. In
March, after six months of Seattle, we were called
back to the San Francisco office. Business results were
better, Carl's salary was raised considerably, but
there were still separations.

CHAPTER IV

On July 3, the Marvelous Son was born, and never was there such a father. Even the trained nurse, hardened to new fathers by years of experience, admitted that she never had seen any one take parenthood quite so hard. Four times in the night he crept in to see if the baby was surely breathing. We were in a very quiet neighborhood, yet the next day, being Fourth of July, now and then a pop would be heard. At each report of a cap-pistol a block away, Carl would dash out and vehemently protest to a group of scornful youngsters that they would wake our son. As if a one-day-old baby would seriously consider waking if a giant fire-cracker went off under his bed!

. Those were magic days. Three of us in the family instead of two — and separations harder than ever. Once in all the ten and a half years we were married I saw Carl Parker downright discouraged over his own affairs, and that was the day I met him down town in Oakland and he announced that he just could not stand the bond business any longer. He had come to dislike it heartily as a business; and then, leaving the boy and me was not worth the whole financial world put together. Since his European experience, — meeting the Webbs and their kind, — he had had a hankering for University work, but he felt that the money return was so small he simply could not contemplate raising a family on it. But now we were desperate.

We longed for a life that would give us the maximum chance to be together. Cold-bloodedly we decided that University work would give us that opportunity, and the long vacations would give us our mountains.

The work itself made its strong appeal, too. Professor Henry Morse Stephens and Professor Miller of the University of California had long urged Carl to go into teaching; and at last we decided that, even if it meant living on husks and skimmed milk all our days, at least we would be eating what there was to eat together, three meals a day every day. We cashed in our savings, we drew on everything there was to draw on, and on February 1, 1909, the three of us embarked for Harvard — with fifty-six dollars and seventy-five cents excess-baggage to pay at the depot, such young ignoramuses we were.

That trip East was worth any future hardship we might have reaped. Our seven-months-old baby was one of the young saints of the world — not once in the five days did he peep. We'd pin him securely in the lower berth of our compartment for his nap, and back we would fly to the corner of the rear platform of the observation car, and gloat, just gloat, over how we had come into the inheritance of all creation. We owned the world. And I, who had never been farther from my California home town than Seattle, who never had seen real snow, except that Christmas when we spent four days at the Scenic Hot Springs in the Cascades, and skied and sledded and spilled around like six-year-olds! But stretches and stretches of snow! And then, just traveling, and together!

And to be in Boston! We took a room with a bath in the Copley Square Hotel. The first evening we arrived, Nandy (Carleton, Jr.) rolled off the bed; so when we went gallivanting about Boston, shopping for the new home, we left him in the bath-tub where he could not fall out. We padded it well with pillows, there was a big window letting in plenty of fresh air, and we instructed the chambermaid to peep at him now and then. And there we would leave him, well-nourished and asleep. (By the time that story had been passed around by enough people in the home town, it developed that one day the baby — just seven months old, remember — got up and turned on the water, and was found by the chambermaid sinking for the third time.)

Something happened to the draft from the home bank, which should have reached Boston almost at the same time we did. We gazed into the family pocket-book one fine morning, to find it, to all intents and purposes, empty. Hurried meeting of the finance committee. By unanimous consent of all present, we decided — as many another mortal in a strange town has decided — on the pawnshop. I wonder if my dear grandmother will read this — she probably will. Carl first submitted his gold watch — the baby had dropped it once, and it had shrunk thereby in the eyes of the pawnshop man, though not in ours. The only other valuable we had along with us was my grandmother's wedding present to me, which had been my grandfather's wedding present to her — a glorious old-fashioned breast-pin. We were allowed fifty dollars on it, which saved the day. What will my grand-mother say when she knows that her bridal gift re-sided for some days in a Boston pawnshop?

We moved out to Cambridge in due time, and set-tled at Bromley Court, on the very edge of the Yard. We thrilled to all of it — we drank in every ounce of dignity and tradition the place afforded, and our wild Western souls exulted. We knew no one when we reached Boston, but our first Sunday we were invited to dinner in Cambridge by two people who were, ever after, our cordial, faithful friends — Mr. and Mrs. John Graham Brooks. They made us feel at once that Cambridge was not the socially icy place it is painted in song and story. Then I remember the afternoon that I had a week's wash strung on an improvised line back and forth from one end of our apartment to the other. Just as I hung the last damp garment, the bell rang, and there stood an immaculate gentleman in a cutaway and silk hat, who had come to call — an old friend of my mother's. He ducked under wet clothes, and we set two chairs where we could see each other, and yet nothing was dripping down either of our necks; and there we conversed, and he ended by in-viting us both to dinner — on Marlborough Street, at that! He must have loved my mother very dearly to have sought further acquaintance with folk who hung the family wash in the hall and the living-room and dining-room. His house on Marlborough Street! We boldly and excitedly figured up on the way home, that they spent on the one meal they fed us more than it cost us to live for two weeks — they honestly did.

Then there was the dear "Jello" lady at the market. I wish she would somehow happen to read this, so as to know that we have never forgotten her. Every Saturday the three of us went to the market, and there was the Jello lady with her samples. The helpings she dished for us each time! She brought the man to whom she was engaged to call on us just before we left. I wonder if they got married, and where they are, and if she still remembers us. She used to say she just waited for Saturdays and our coming. Then there was dear Granny Jones, who kept a boarding-house half a block away. I do not remember how we came to know her, but some good angel saw to it. She used to send around little bowls of luscious dessert, and half a pie, or some hot muffins. Then I was always grateful also — for it made such a good story, and it was true — to the New England wife of a fellow graduate student who remarked, when I told her we had one baby and another on the way, "How interesting — just like the slums!"

We did our own work, of course, and we lived on next to nothing. I wonder now how we kept so well that year. Of course, we fed the baby everything he should have, — according to Holt in those days, — and we ate the mutton left from his broth and the beef after the juice had been squeezed out of it for him, and bought storage eggs ourselves, and queer butter out of a barrel, and were absolutely, absolutely blissful. Perhaps we should have spent more on food and less on baseball. I am glad we did not. Almost every Saturday afternoon that first semester we fared forth early, Nandy in his go-cart, to get a seat in the front row of the baseball grandstand. I remember one Saturday we were late, front seats all taken. We had to pack baby and go-cart more than half-way up to the top. There we barricaded him, still in the go-cart, in the middle of the aisle. Along about the seventh inning, the game waxed particularly exciting — we were beside ourselves with enthusiasm. Fellow onlookers seemed even more excited — they called out things — they seemed to be calling in our direction. Fine parents we were — there was Nandy, go-cart and all, bumpety-bumping down the grandstand steps.

I remember again the Stadium on the day of the big track meet. Every time the official announcer would put the megaphone to his mouth, to call out winners and time to a hushed and eager throng, Nandy, not yet a year old, would begin to squeal at the top of his lungs for joy. Nobody could hear a word the official said. We were as distressed as any one — we, too, had pencils poised to jot down records.

Carl studied very hard. The first few weeks, until we got used to the new wonder of things, he used to run home from college whenever he had a spare minute, just to be sure he was that near. At that time he was rather preparing to go into Transportation as his main economic subject. But by the end of the year he knew Labor would be his love. (His first published economic article was a short one that appeared in the "Quarterly Journal of Economics" for May, 1910, on "The Decline of Trade-Union Membership.") We had a tragic summer.

Carl felt that he must take his Master's degree, but he had no foreign language. Three terrible, wicked, unforgivable professors assured him that, if he could be in Germany six weeks during summer vacation, he could get enough German to pass the examination for the A.M. We believed them, and he went; though of all the partings we ever had, that was the very worst. Almost at the last he just could not go; but we were so sure that it would solve the whole A.M. problem. He went third class on a German steamer, since we had money for nothing better. The food did distress even his unfinicky soul. After a particularly sad offering of salt herring, uncooked, on a particularly rough day, he wrote, "I find I am not a good Hamburger German. The latter eat all things in all weather."

Oh, the misery of that summer! We never talked about it much. He went to Freiburg, to a German cobbler's family, but later changed, as the cobbler's son looked upon him as a dispensation of Providence, sent to practise his English upon. His heart was breaking, and mine was breaking, and he was working at German (and languages came fearfully hard for him) morning, afternoon, and night, with two lessons a day, his only diversion being a daily walk up a hill, with a cake of soap and a towel, to a secluded waterfall he discovered. He wrote a letter and a postcard a day to the babe and me. I have just re-read all of them, and my heart aches afresh for the homesickness that summer meant to both of us.

He got back two days before our wedding anniversary — days like those first few after our reunion are not given to many mortals. I would say no one had ever tasted such joy. The baby gurgled about, and was kissed within an inch of his life. The Jello lady sent around a dessert of sixteen different colors, more or less, big enough for a family of eight, as her welcome home.

About six weeks later we called our beloved Dr. J—— from a banquet he had long looked forward to, in order to officiate at the birth of our second, known as Thomas-Elizabeth up to October 17, but from about ten-thirty that night as James Stratton Parker. We named him after my grandfather, for the simple reason that we liked the name Jim. How we chuckled when my father's congratulatory telegram came, in which he claimed pleasure at having the boy named after his father, but cautioned us never to allow him to be nicknamed. I remember the boresome youth who used to call, week in week out, — always just before a meal, — and we were so hard up, and got so that we resented feeding such an impossible person so many times. He dropped in at noon Friday the 17th, for lunch. A few days later Carl met him on the street and announced rapturously the arrival of the new son. The impossible person hemmed and stammered: "Why — er — when did it arrive?" Carl, all beams, replied, "The very evening of the day you were at our house for lunch!" We never laid eyes on that man again! We were almost four months longer in Cambridge, but never did he step foot inside our apartment. I wish some one could have psycho-analyzed him, but it's too late now. He died about a year after we left Cambridge. I always felt that he never got over the shock of having escaped Jim's arrival by such a narrow margin.

And right here I must tell of Dr. J——. He was recommended as the best doctor in Cambridge, but very expensive. "We may have to economize in everything on earth," said Carl, "but we'll never economize on doctors." So we had Dr. J——, had him for all the minor upsets that families need doctors for; had him when Jim was born; had him through a queer fever Nandy developed that lasted some time; had him through a bad case of grippe I got (this was at Christmastime, and Carl took care of both babies, did all the cooking, even to the Christmas turkey I was well enough to eat by then, got up every two hours for three nights to change an ice-pack I had to have — that's the kind of man he was!); had him vaccinate both children; and then, just before we left Cambridge, we sat and held his bill, afraid to open the envelope. At length we gathered our courage, and gazed upon charges of sixty-five dollars for everything, with a wonderful note which said that, if we would be inconvenienced in paying that, he would not mind at all if he got nothing.

Such excitement! We had expected two hundred dollars at the least! We tore out and bought ten cents' worth of doughnuts, to celebrate. When we exclaimed to him over his goodness, — of course we paid the sixty-five dollars, — all he said was: "Do you think a doctor is blind? And does a man go steerage to Europe if he has a lot of money in the bank?" Bless that doctor's heart! Bless all doctors' hearts! We went through our married life in the days of our financial slimness, with kindness shown us by every doctor we ever had. I remember our Heidelberg German doctor sent us a bill for a year of a dollar and a half. And even in our more prosperous days, at Carl's last illness, with that good Seattle doctor calling day and night, and caring for me after Carl's death, he refused to send any bill for anything. And a little later, when I paid a long overdue bill to our blessed Oakland doctor for a tonsil operation, he sent the check back torn in two. Bless doctors!

When we left for Harvard, we had an idea that perhaps one year of graduate work would be sufficient. Naturally, about two months was enough to show us that one year would get us nowhere. Could we finance an added year at, perhaps, Wisconsin? And then, in November, Professor Miller of Berkeley called to talk things over with Carl. Anon he remarked, more or less casually, "The thing for you to do is to have a year's study in Germany," and proceeded to enlarge on that idea. We sat dumb, and the minute the door was closed after him, we flopped. "What was the man thinking of — to suggest a year in Germany, when we have no money and two babies, one not a year and a half, and one six weeks old!" Preposterous!

That was Saturday afternoon. By Monday morning we had decided we would go! Thereupon we wrote West to finance the plan, and got beautifully sat upon for our "notions." If we needed money, we had better give up this whole fool University idea and get a decent man-sized job. And then we wrote my father, — or, rather, I wrote him without telling Carl till after the letter was mailed, — and bless his heart! he replied with a fat God-bless-you-my-children registered letter, with check enclosed, agreeing to my stipulation that it should be a six-per-cent business affair. Suppose we could not have raised that money — suppose our lives had been minus that German experience! Bless fathers! They may scold and fuss at romance, and have "good sensible ideas of their own" on such matters, but — bless fathers!

CHAPTER V

WE finished our year at Harvard, giving up the A.M. idea for the present. Carl got A's in every subject and was asked to take a teaching fellowship under Ripley; but it was Europe for us. We set forth February 22, 1909, in a big snowstorm, with two babies, and one thousand six hundred and seventy-six bundles, bags, and presents. Jim was in one of those fur-bags that babies use in the East. Everything we were about to forget the last minute got shoved into that bag with Jim, and it surely began to look as if we had brought a young and very lumpy mastodon into the world!

We went by boat from Boston to New York, and sailed on the Pennsylvania February 24. People wrote us in those days: "You two brave people — think of starting to Europe with two babies!" Brave was the last word to use. Had we worried or had fears over anything, and yet fared forth, we should perhaps have been brave. As it was, I can feel again the sensation of leaving New York, gazing back on the city buildings and bridges bathed in sunshine after the storm. Exultant joy was in our hearts, that was all. Not one worry, not one concern, not one small drop of homesickness. We were to see Europe together, years before we had dreamed it possible. It just seemed too glorious to be true. "Brave"? Far from it. Simply eager, glowing, filled to the brim with a determination to drain every day to the full.

I discovered that, while my husband had married a
female who could not cook rice (though she learned),
I had taken unto myself a spouse who curled up green
half a day out on the ocean, and stayed that way for
about six days. He tried so desperately to help with
the babies, but it always made matters worse. If I had
turned green, too — But babies and I prospered without interruption, though some ants did try to eat
Jim's scalp off one night — "sugar ants" the doctor
called them. "They knew their business," our dad remarked. We were three days late getting into Hamburg — fourteen days on the ocean, all told. And then
to be in Hamburg — in Germany — in Europe! I remember our first meal in the queer little cheap hotel
we rooted out. *"Eier"* was the only word on the bill
of fare we could make out, so Carl brushed up his
German and ordered four for us, fried. And the waiter
brought four each. He probably declared for years
that all Americans always eat four fried eggs each
and every night for supper.

We headed for Leipzig at once, and there Carl
unearthed the Pension Schröter on Sophien Platz.
There we had two rooms and all the food we could eat,
— far too much for us to eat, and oh! so delicious, —
for fifty-five dollars a month for the entire family, although Jim hardly ranked as yet, economically speak-
ing, as part of the consuming public. We drained
Leipzig to the dregs — a good German idiom. Carl
worked at his German steadily, almost frantically, with
a lesson every day along with all his university work
— a seven o'clock lecture by Bücher every morning

being the cheery start for the day, and we blocks and blocks from the University. I think of Carl through those days with extra pride, though it is hard to decide that I was ever prouder of him at one time than another. But he strained and labored without ceasing at such an uninspiring job. All his hard study that broken-hearted summer at Freiburg had given him no single word of an economic vocabulary. In Leipzig he listened hour by hour to the lectures of his German professors, sometimes not understanding an important word for several days, yet exerting every intellectual muscle to get some light in his darkness. Then, for hours each day and almost every evening, it was grammar, grammar, grammar, till he wondered at times if all life meant an understanding of the subjunctive. Then, little by little, rays of hope. "I caught five words in ——'s lecture to-day!" Then it was ten, then twenty. Never a lecture of any day did he miss.

We stole moments for joy along the way. First, of course, there was the opera — grand opera at twenty-five cents a seat. How Wagner bored us at first — except the parts here and there that we had known all our lives. Neither of us had had any musical education to speak of; each of us got great joy out of what we considered "good" music, but which was evidently low-brow. And Wagner at first was too much for us. That night in Leipzig we heard the "Walküre!" — utterly aghast and rather impatient at so much non-understandable noise. Then we would drop down to "Carmen," "La Bohême," Hoffman's "Erzählung," and think, "This is life!" Each night that we spared for a spree we sought out some beer-hall — as unfrequented a one as possible, to get all the local color we could.

Once Carl decided that, as long as we had come so far, I must get a glimpse of real European night-life — it might startle me a bit, but would do no harm. So, after due deliberation, he led me to the Café Bauer, the reputed wild and questionable resort of Leipzig night-life, though the pension glanced ceiling-wards and sighed and shook their heads. I do not know just what I did expect to see, but I know that what I saw was countless stolid family parties — on all sides grandmas and grandpas and sons and daughters, and the babies in high chairs beating the tables with spoons. It was quite the most moral atmosphere we ever found ourselves in. That is what you get for deliberately setting out to see the wickedness of the world!

From Leipzig we went to Berlin. We did not want to go to Berlin — Jena was the spot we had in mind. Just as a few months at Harvard showed us that one year there would be but a mere start, so one semester in Germany showed us that one year there would get us nowhere. We must stay longer, — from one to two years longer, — but how, alas, how finance it? That eternal question! We finally decided that, if we took the next semester or so in Berlin, Carl could earn money enough coaching to keep us going without having to borrow more. So to Berlin we went. We accomplished our financial purpose, but at too great a cost.

In Berlin we found a small furnished apartment on the ground floor of a Gartenhaus in Charlottenburg — Mommsen Strasse it was. At once Carl started out to find coaching; and how he found it always seemed to me an illustration of the way he could succeed at anything anywhere. We knew no one in Berlin. First he went to the minister of the American church; he in turn gave him names of Americans who might want coaching, and then Carl looked up those people. In about two months he had all the coaching he could possibly handle, and we could have stayed indefinitely in Berlin in comfort, for Carl was making over one hundred dollars a month, and that in his spare time.

But the agony of those months: to be in Germany and yet get so little Germany out of it! We had splendid letters of introduction to German people, from German friends we had made in Leipzig, but we could not find a chance even to present them. Carl coached three youngsters in the three R's; he was preparing two of the age just above, for college; he had one American youth, who had ambitions to burst out monthly in the "Saturday Evening Post" stories; there was a class of five middle-aged women, who wanted Shakespeare, and got it; two classes in Current Events; one group of Christian Scientists, who put in a modest demand for the history of the world. I remember Carl had led them up to Pepin the Short when we left Berlin. He contracted everything and anything except one group who desired a course of lectures on Pragmatism. I do not think he had ever heard of the term then, but he took one look at the lay of the land and said — not so! In his last years, when he became such a worshiper at the shrine of William James and John Dewey, we often used to laugh at his Berlin profanity over the very idea of ever getting a word of such "bunk" into his head.

But think of the strain it all meant — lessons and lessons every day, on every subject under heaven, and in every spare minute continued grinding at his German, and, of course, every day numerous hours at the University, and so little time for sprees together. We assumed in our prosperity the luxury of a maid — the unparalleled Anna Bederke aus Rothenburg, Kreis Bumps (?), Posen, at four dollars a month, who for a year and a half was the amusement and desperation of ourselves and our friends. Dear, crooked-nosed, one-good-eye Anna! She adored the ground we walked on. Our German friends told us we had ruined her forever — she would never be fit for the discipline of a German household again. Since war was first declared we have lost all track of Anna. Was her Poland home in the devastated country? Did she marry a soldier, and is she too, perhaps, a widow? Faithful Anna, do not think for one minute you will ever be forgotten by the Parkers.

With Anna to leave the young with now and then, I was able to get in two sprees a week with Carl. Every Wednesday and Saturday noon I met him at the University and we had lunch together. Usually on Wednesdays we ate at the Café Rheingold, the spot I think of with most affection as I look back on Berlin.

We used to eat in the "Shell Room" — an individual chicken-and-rice pie (as much chicken as rice), a vegetable, and a glass of beer each, for thirty-five cents for both. Saturdays we hunted for different smaller out-of-the-way restaurants. Wednesday nights "Uncle K." of the University of Wisconsin always came to supper, bringing a thirty-five-cent rebate his landlady allowed him when he ate out; and we had chicken every Wednesday night, which cost — a fat one — never more than fifty cents. (It was Uncle K. who wrote, "The world is so different with Carl gone!") Once we rented bicycles and rode all through the Tiergarten, Carl and I, with the expected stiffness and soreness next day.

Then there was Christmas in Berlin. Three friends traveled up from Rome to be with us, two students came from Leipzig, and four from Berlin — eleven for dinner, and four chairs all told. It was a regular "La Bohême" festival — one guest appearing with a bottle of wine under his arm, another with a jar of caviare sent him from Russia. We had a gay week of it after Christmas, when the whole eleven of us went on some Dutch-treat spree every night, before going back to our studies.

Then came those last grueling months in Berlin, when Carl had a breakdown, and I got sick nursing him and had to go to a German hospital; and while I was there Jim was threatened with pneumonia and Nandy got tonsillitis. In the midst of it all the lease expired on our Wohnung, and Carl and Anna had to move the family out. We decided that we had had all we wanted of coaching in Berlin, — we came to that conclusion before any of the breakdowns, — threw our pride to the winds, borrowed more money from my good father, and as soon as the family was well enough to travel, we made for our ever-to-be-adored Heidelberg.

CHAPTER VI

HERE I sit back, and words fail me. I see that year as a kaleidoscope of one joyful day after another, each rushing by and leaving the memory that we both always had, of the most perfect year that was ever given to mortals on earth. I remember our eighth wedding anniversary in Berkeley. We had been going night after night until we were tired of going anywhere, — engagements seemed to have heaped up, — so we decided that the very happiest way we could celebrate that most-to-be-celebrated of all dates was just to stay at home, plug the telephone, pull down the blinds, and have an evening by ourselves. Then we got out everything that we kept as mementos of our European days, and went over them — all the post-cards, memory-books, theatre and opera programmes, etc., and, lastly, read my diary — I had kept a record of every day in Europe. When we came to that year in Heidelberg, we just could not believe our own eyes. How had we ever managed to pack a year so full, and live to tell the tale? I wish I could write a story of just that year. We swore an oath in Berlin that we would make Heidelberg mean Germany to us — no English-speaking, no Americans. As far as it lay in our power, we lived up to it. Carl and I spoke only German to each other and to the children, and we shunned our fellow countrymen as if they had had the plague. And Carl, in the characteristic way he had, set out to fill our lives with all the real German life we could get into them, not waiting for that life to come of itself — which it might never have done.

One afternoon, on his way home from the University, he discovered in a back alley the Weiser Boch, a little restaurant and beer-hall so full of local color that it "hollered." No, it did not holler: it was too real for that. It was sombre and carved up — it whispered. Carl made immediate friends, in the way he had, with the portly Frau and Herr who ran the Weiser Boch: they desired to meet me, they desired to see the Kinder, and would not the Herr Student like to have the Weiser Boch lady mention his name to some of the German students who dropped in? Carl left his card, and wondered if anything would come of it.

The very next afternoon, — such a glowing account of the Amerikaner the Weiser Boch lady must have given, — a real truly German student, in his corps cap and ribbons, called at our home — the stiffest, most decorous heel-clicking German student I ever was to see. His embarrassment was great when he discovered that Carl was out, and I seemed to take it quite for granted that he was to sit down for a moment and visit with me. He fell over everything. But we visited, and I was able to gather that his corps wished Herr Student Par-r-r-ker to have beer with them the following evening. Then he bowed himself backwards and out, and fled.

I could scarce wait for Carl to get home — it was too good to be true. And that was but the beginning.

Invitation after invitation came to Carl, first from one corps, then from another; almost every Saturday night he saw German student-life first hand somewhere, and at least one day a week he was invited to the duels in the Hirsch Gasse. Little by little we got the students to our Wohnung; then we got chummier and chummier, till we would walk up Haupt Strasse saluting here, passing a word there, invited to some student function one night, another affair another night. The students who lived in Heidelberg had us meet their families, and those who were batching in Heidelberg often had us come to their rooms. We made friendships during that year that nothing could ever mar.

It is two years now since we received the last letter from any Heidelberg chum. Are they all killed, perhaps? And when we can communicate again, after the war, think of what I must write them! Carl was a revelation to most of them — they would talk about him to me, and ask if all Americans were like him, so fresh in spirit, so clean, so sincere, so full of fun, and, with it all, doing the finest work of all of them but one in the University.

The economics students tried to think of some way of influencing Alfred Weber to give another course of lectures at the University. He was in retirement at Heidelberg, but still the adored of the students. Finally, they decided that a committee of three should represent them and make a personal appeal. Carl was one of the three chosen. The report soon flew around, how, in Weber's august presence, the Amerikaner had stood with his hands in his pockets — even sat for a few moments on the edge of Weber's desk. The two Germans, posed like ramrods, expected to see such informality shoved out bodily. Instead, when they took their leave, the Herr Professor had actually patted the Amerikaner on the shoulder, and said he guessed he would give the lectures.

Then his report in Gothein's Seminar, which went so well that I fairly burst with pride. He had worked day and night on that. I was to meet him at eight after it had been given, and we were to have a celebration. I was standing by the entrance to the University building when out came an enthused group of jabbering German students, Carl in their midst. They were patting him on the back, shaking his hands furiously; and when they saw me, they rushed to tell me of Carl's success and how Gothein had said before all that it had been the best paper presented that semester.

I find myself smiling as I write this — I was too happy that night to eat.

The Sunday trips we made up the Neckar: each morning early we would take the train and ride to where we had walked the Sunday previous; then we would tramp as far as we could, — meaning until dark, — have lunch at some untouristed inn along the road, or perhaps eat a picnic lunch of our own in some old castle ruin, and then ride home. Oh, those Sundays! I tell you no two people in all this world, since people were, have ever had *one* day like those Sundays. And we had them almost every week. It would have been worth going to Germany for just one of those days.

There was the gay, glad party that the Economic students gave, out in Handschusheim at the "zum Bachlenz"; first, the banquet, with a big roomful of jovial young Germans; then the play, in which Carl and I both took part. Carl appeared in a mixture of his Idaho outfit and a German peasant's costume, beating a large drum. He represented "Materialindex," and called out loudly, "Ich bitte mich nicht zu vergessen. Ich bin auch da." I was "Methode," which nobody wanted to claim; whereat I wept. I am looking at the flashlight picture of us all at this moment. Then came the dancing, and then at about four o'clock the walk home in the moonlight, by the old castle ruin in Handschusheim, singing the German student-songs.

There was Carnival season, with its masque balls and frivolity, and Faschings Dienstag, when Hauptstrasse was given over to merriment all afternoon, every one trailing up and down the middle of the street masked, and in fantastic costume, throwing confetti and tooting horns, Carl and I tooting with the rest.

As time went on, we came to have one little group of nine students whom we were with more than any others. As each of the men took his degree, he gave a party to the rest of us to celebrate it, every one trying to outdo the other in fun. Besides these most important degree celebrations, there were less dazzling affairs, such as birthday parties, dinners, or afternoon coffee in honor of visiting German parents, or merely meeting together in our favorite café after a Socialist lecture or a Max Reger concert. In addition to such functions, Carl and I had our Wednesday night spree just by ourselves, when every week we met after his seminar. Our budget allowed just twelve and a half cents an evening for both of us. I put up a supper at home, and in good weather we ate down by the river or in some park. When it rained and was cold, we sat in a corner of the third-class waiting-room by the stove, watching the people coming and going in the station. Then, for dessert, we went every Wednesday to Tante's Conditorei, where, for two and a half cents apiece, we got a large slice of a special brand of the most divine cake ever baked. Then, for two and a half cents, we saw the movies — at a reduced rate because we presented a certain number of street-car transfers along with the cash, and then had to sit in the first three rows. But you see, we used to remark, we have to sit so far away at the opera, it's good to get up close at something! Those were real movies — no danger of running into a night-long Robert W. Chambers scenario. It was in the days before such developments. Then across the street was an "Automat," and there, for a cent and a quarter apiece, we could hold a glass under a little spigot, press a button, and get — refreshments. Then we walked home.

O Heidelberg — I love your every tree, every stone, every blade of grass!

But at last our year came to an end. We left the town in a bower of fruit-blossoms, as we had found it.

Our dear, most faithful friends, the Kecks, gave us a farewell luncheon; and with babies, bundles, and baggage, we were off.

Heidelberg was the only spot I ever wept at leaving. I loved it then, and I love it now, as I love no other place on earth and Carl felt the same way. We were mournful, indeed, as that train pulled out.

CHAPTER VII

THE next two weeks were filled with vicissitudes. The idea was for Carl to settle the little family in some rural bit of Germany, while he did research work in the industrial section of Essen, and thereabouts, coming home week-ends. We stopped off first at Bonn. Carl spent several days searching up and down the Rhine and through the Moselle country for a place that would do, which meant a place we could afford that was fit and suitable for the babies. There was nothing. The report always was: pensions all expensive, and automobiles touring by at a mile a minute where the children would be playing.

On a wild impulse we moved up to Clive, on the Dutch border. After Carl went in search of a pension, it started to drizzle. The boys, baggage, and I found the only nearby place of shelter in a stone-cutter's inclosure, filled with new and ornate tombstones. What was my impecunious horror, when I heard a small crash and discovered that Jim had dislocated a loose figure of Christ (unconsciously Cubist in execution) from the top of a tombstone! Eight marks charges! the cost of sixteen Heidelberg sprees. On his return, Carl reported two pensions, one quarantined for diphtheria, one for scarlet fever. We slept over a beer-hall, with such a racket going on all night as never was; and next morning took the first train out — this time for Düsseldorf.

It is a trifle momentous, traveling with two babies around a country you know nothing about, and can find no one to enlighten you. At Düsseldorf Carl searched through the town and suburbs for a spot to settle us in, getting more and more depressed at the thought of leaving us anywhere. That Freiburg summer had seared us both deep, and each of us dreaded another separation more than either let the other know. And then, one night, after another fruit-less search, Carl came home and informed me that the whole scheme was off. Instead of doing his research work, we would all go to Munich, and he would take an unexpected semester there, working with Brentano.

What rejoicings, oh, what rejoicings! As Carl re-marked, it may be that "He travels fastest who trav-els alone"; but speed was not the only thing he was after. So the next day, babies, bundles, baggage, and parents went down the Rhine, almost through Heidelberg, to Munich, with such joy and content-ment in our hearts as we could not describe. All those days of unhappy searchings Carl had been through must have sunk deep, for in his last days of fever he would tell me of a form of delirium in which he searched again, with a heart of lead, for a place to leave the babies and me.

I remember our first night in Munich. We arrived about supper-time, hunted up a cheap hotel as usual, near the station, fed the babies, and started to pre-pare for their retirement. This process in hotels was always effected by taking out two bureau-drawers and making a bed of each. While we were busy over

this, the boys were busy over — just busy. This time
they both crawled up into a large clothes-press that
stood in our room, when, crash! bang! — there lay the
clothes-press, front down, on the floor, boys inside it.
Such a commotion — hollerings and squallings from
the internals of the clothes-press, agitated scurryings
from all directions of the hotel-keeper, his wife, waiters, and chambermaids. All together, we managed to
stand the clothes-press once more against the wall,
and to extricate two sobered young ones, the only
damage being two clothes-press doors banged off their
hinges.

Munich is second in my heart to Heidelberg. Carl
worked hardest of all there, hardly ever going out
nights; but we never got over the feeling that our
being there together was a sort of gift we had made
ourselves, and we were ever grateful. And then Carl
did so remarkably well in the University. A report,
for instance, which he read before Brentano's seminar
was published by the University. Our relations with
Brentano always stood out as one of the high memories of Germany. After Carl's report in Brentano's
class, that lovable idol of the German students called
him to his desk and had a long talk, which ended by
his asking us both to tea at his house the following
day. The excitement of our pension over that! We
were looked upon as the anointed of the Lord. We
were really a bit overawed, ourselves. We discussed
neckties, and brushed and cleaned, and smelled considerably of gasoline as we strutted forth, too proud
to tell, because we were to have tea with Brentano!

I can see the street their house was on, their front door; I can feel again the little catch in our breaths as we rang the bell. Then the charming warmth and color of that Italian home, the charming warmth and hospitality of that white-haired professor and his gracious, kindly wife. There were just ourselves there; and what a momentous time it was to the little Parkers! Carl was simply radiating joy, and in the way he always had when especially pleased, would give a sudden beam from ear to ear, and a wink at me when no one else was looking.

Not long after that we were invited for dinner, and again for tea, this time, according to orders, bringing the sons. They both fell into an Italian fountain in the rear garden as soon as we went in for refreshments. By my desk now is hanging a photograph we have prized as one of our great treasures. Below it is written: "Mrs. and Mr. Parker, zur freundlichen Erinnerrung — Lujio Brentano." Professor Bonn, another of Carl's professors at the University, and his wife, were kindness itself to us. Then there was Peter, dear old Peter, the Austrian student at our pension, who took us everywhere, brought us gifts, and adored the babies until he almost spoiled them.

From Munich we went direct to England. Vicissitudes again in finding a cheap and fit place that would do for children to settle in. After ever-hopeful wanderings, we finally stumbled upon Swanage in Dorset. That was a love of a place on the English Channel, where we had two rooms with the Mebers in their funny little brick house, the "Netto." Simple folk they were: Mr. Meber a retired sailor, the wife rather worn with constant roomers, one daughter a dressmaker, the other working in the "knittin'" shop. Charges, six dollars a week for the family, which included cooking and serving our meals — we bought the food ourselves.

Here Carl prepared for his Ph.D. examination, and worked on his thesis until it got to the point where he needed the British Museum. Then he took a room and worked during the week in London, coming down to us week-ends. He wrote eager letters, for the time had come when he longed to get the preparatory work and examination behind him and begin teaching. We had an instructorship at the University of California waiting for us, and teaching was to begin in January. In one letter he wrote: "I now feel like landing on my exam. like a Bulgarian; I am that fierce to lay it out." We felt more than ever, in those days of work piling up behind us, that we owned the world; as Carl wrote in another letter: "We'll stick this out [this being the separation of his last trip to London, whence he was to start for Heidelberg and his examination, without another visit with us], for, *Gott sei dank!* the time is n't so fearful, fearful long, it is n't really, is it? Gee! I'm glad I married you. And I want more babies and more you, and then the whole gang together for about ninety-two years. But life is so fine to us and we are getting so much love and big things out of life!"

November 1 Carl left London for Heidelberg. He was to take his examination there December 5, so the month of November was a full one for him. He stayed with the dear Kecks, Mother Keck pressing and mending his clothes, hovering over him as if he were her own son. He wrote once: "To-day we had a small leg of venison which I sneaked in last night. Every time I note that I burn three quarters of a lampful of oil a day among the other things I cost them, it makes me feel like buying out a whole Conditorei."

I lived for those daily letters telling of his progress. Once he wrote: "Just saw Fleiner [Professor in Law] and he was *fine*, but I must get his Volkerrecht cold. It is fine reading, and is mighty good and interesting every word, and also stuff which a man ought to know. This is the last man to see. From now on, it is only to *study*, and I am tickled. I do really like to study." A few days later he wrote: "It is just plain sit and absorb these days. Some day I will explain how tough it is to learn an entire law subject in five days in a strange tongue."

And then, on the night of December 5, came the telegram of success to "Frau Dr. Parker." We both knew he would pass, but neither of us was prepared for the verdict of "*Summa cum laude*," the highest accomplishment possible. I went up and down the main street of little Swanage, announcing the tidings right and left. The community all knew that Carl was in Germany to take some kind of an examination, though it all seemed rather unexplainable. Yet they rejoiced with me, — the butcher, the baker, the candlestick-maker, — without having the least idea what they were rejoicing about. Mrs. Meber tore up and down Osborne Road to have the fun of telling the immediate neighbors, all of whom were utterly at a loss to know what it meant, the truth being that Mrs. Meber herself was in that same state. But she had somehow caught my excitement, and anything to tell was scarce in Swanage.

So the little family that fared forth from Oakland, California, that February 1, for one year at Harvard had ended thus — almost four years later a Ph.D. *summa cum laude* from Heidelberg. Not Persia as we had planned it nine years before — a deeper, finer life than anything we had dreamed. We asked Professor Miller, after we got back to California, why in the world he had said just "one year in Europe."

"If I had said more, I was afraid it would scare you altogether out of ever starting; and I knew if you once got over there and were made of the right stuff, you'd stay on for a Ph.D."

On December 12 Carl was to deliver one of a series of lectures in Munich for the Handelshochschule, his subject being "Die Einwanderungs und Siedelungspolitik in Amerika (Carleton Parker, Privatdocent, California-Universität, St. Francisco)." That very day, however, the Prince Regent died, and everything was called off. We had our glory — and got our pay. Carl was so tired from his examination, that he did not object to foregoing the delivery of a German address before an audience of four hundred. It was read two weeks later by one of the professors.

On December 15 we had our reunion and celebration of it all. Carl took the Amerika, second class, at Hamburg; the boys and I at Southampton, ushered thither from Swanage and put aboard the steamer by our faithful Onkel Keck, son of the folk with whom Carl had stayed in Heidelberg, who came all the way from London for that purpose. It was not such a brash Herr Doktor that we found, after all: the Channel had begun to tell on him, as it were, and while it was plain that he loved us, it was also plain that he did not love the water. So we gave him his six days off, and he lay anguish-eyed in a steamer-chair while I covered fifty-seven miles a day, tearing after two sons who were far more filled with Wander-lust than they had been three years before. When our dad did feel chipper again, he felt very chipper, and our last four days were perfect.

We landed in New York on Christmas Eve, in a snowstorm; paid the crushing sum of one dollar and seventy-five cents duty, — such a jovial agent as in-spected our belongings I never beheld; he must al-ready have had just the Christmas present he most wanted, whatever it was. When he heard that we had been in Heidelberg, he and several other offi-cials began a lusty rendering of "Old Heidelberg," — and within an hour we were speeding toward Cali-fornia, a case of certified milk added to our already innumerable articles of luggage. Christmas dinner we ate on the train. How those American dining-car prices floored us after three years of all we could eat for thirty-five cents!

CHAPTER VIII

WE looked back always on our first semester's teaching in the University of California as one hectic term. We had lived our own lives, found our own joys, for four years, and here we were enveloped by old friends, by relatives, by new friends, until we knew not which way to turn. In addition, Carl was swamped by campus affairs — by students, many of whom seemed to consider him an oasis in a desert of otherwise-to-be-deplored, unhuman professors. Every student organization to which he had belonged as an undergraduate opened its arms to welcome him as a faculty member; we chaperoned student parties till we heard rag-time in our sleep. From January 1 to May 16, we had four nights alone together. You can know we were desperate. Carl used to say: "We may have to make it Persia yet."

The red-letter event of that term was when, after about two months of teaching, President Wheeler rang up one evening about seven, — one of the four evenings, as it happened, we were at home together, — and said: "I thought I should like the pleasure of telling you personally, though you will receive official notice in the morning, that you have been made an assistant professor. We expected you to make good, but we did not expect you to make good to such a degree quite so soon."

Again an occasion for a spree! We tore out hatless

across the campus, nearly demolishing the head of the College of Commerce as we rounded the Library. He must know the excitement. He was pleased. He slipped his hand into his pocket saying, "I must have a hand in this celebration." And with a royal gesture, as who should say, "What matter the costs!" slipped a dime into Carl's hand. "Spend it all to-night."

Thus we were started on our assistant professorship. But always before and always after, to the students Carl was just "Doc."

I remember a story he told of how his chief stopped him one afternoon at the north gate to the university, and said he was discouraged and distressed. Carl was getting the reputation of being popular with the students, and that would never do. "I don't wish to hear more of such rumors." Just then the remnants of the internals of a Ford, hung together with picture wire and painted white, whizzed around the corner. Two slouching, hard-working "studes" caught sight of Carl, reared up the car, and called, "Hi, Doc, come on in!" Then they beheld the Head of the Department, hastily pressed some lever, and went hurrying on. To the Head it was evidence first-hand. He shook his head and went his way.

Carl was popular with the students, and it is true that he was too much so. It was not long before he discovered that he was drawing unto himself the all-too-lightly-handled "college bum," and he rebelled. Harvard and Germany had given him too high an idea of scholarship to have even a traditional university patience with the student who, in the University

of California jargon, was "looking for a meal." He
was petitioned by twelve students of the College of
Agriculture to give a course in the Economics of
Agriculture, and they guaranteed him twenty-five
students. One hundred and thirty enrolled, and as
Carl surveyed the assortment below him, he realized
that a good half of them did not know and did not
want to know a pear tree from a tractor. He stiffened
his upper lip, stiffened his examinations, and cinched
forty of the class. There should be some Latin saying
that would just fit such a case, but I do not know it.
It would start, "Exit ——," and the exit would refer
to the exit of the loafer in large numbers from Carl's
courses and the exit from the heart of the loafer of the
absorbing love he had held for Carl. His troubles were
largely over. Someone else could care for the maimed,
the halt, and the blind.

It was about this time, too, that Carl got into
difficulties with the intrenched powers on the campus.
He had what has been referred to as "a passion for
justice." Daily the injustice of campus organization
grew on him; he saw democracy held high as an ideal
— lip-homage only. Student affairs were run by an
autocracy which had nothing to justify it except its
supporters' claim of "efficiency." He had little love
for that word — it is usually bought at too great a
cost. That year, as usual, he had a small seminar of
carefully picked students. He got them to open their
eyes to conditions as they were. When they ceased to
accept those conditions just because they were, they,
too, felt the inequality, the farce, of a democratic

institution run on such autocratic lines. After seminar hours the group would foregather at our house to plot as to ways and means. The editor of the campus daily saw their point of view — I am not sure now that he was not a member of the seminar.

A slow campaign of education followed. Intrenched powers became outraged. Fraternities that had invited Carl almost weekly to lunch, now "could n't see him." One or two influential alumnæ, who had something to gain from the established order, took up the fight. Soon we had a "warning" from one of the Regents that Carl's efforts on behalf of "democracy" were unwelcome. But within a year the entire organization of campus politics was altered, and now there probably is not a student who would not feel outraged at the suggestion of a return to the old system.

Perhaps here is where I can dwell for a moment on Carl's particular brand of democracy. I see so much of other kinds. He was what I should call an utterly unconscious democrat. He never framed in his own mind any theory of "the brotherhood of man" — he just lived it, without ever thinking of it as something that needed expression in words. I never heard him use the term. To him the Individual was everything — by that I mean that every relation he had was on a personal basis. He could not go into a shop to buy a necktie hurriedly, without passing a word with the clerk; when he paid his fare on the street car, there was a moment's conversation with the conductor; when we had ice-cream of an evening, he asked the waitress what was the best thing on in the movies.

When we left Oakland for Harvard, the partially toothless maid we had sobbed that "Mr. Parker had been more like a brother to her!"

One of the phases of his death which struck home the hardest was the concern and sorrow the small tradespeople showed — the cobbler, the plumber, the drug-store clerk. You hear men say: "I often find it interesting to talk to working-people and get their view-point." Such an attitude was absolutely foreign to Carl. He talked to "working-people" because he talked to everybody as he went along his joyous way. At a track meet or football game, he was on intimate terms with every one within a conversational radius. Our wealthy friends would tell us he ruined their chauffeurs — they got so that they did n't know their places. As likely as not, he would jolt some constrained bank president by engaging him in genial conversation without an introduction; at a formal dinner he would, as a matter of course, have a word or two with the butler when he passed the cracked crab, although at times the butlers seemed somewhat pained thereby. Some of Carl's intimate friends were occasionally annoyed — "He talks to everybody." He no more could help talking to everybody than he could help — liking pumpkin-pie. He was born that way. He had one manner for every human being — President of the University, students, janitors, society women, cooks, small boys, judges. He never had any material thing to hand out, — not even cigars, for he did not smoke himself, — but, as one friend expressed it, "he radiated generosity."

Heidelberg gives one year after passing the examination to get the doctor's thesis in final form for publication. The subject of Carl's thesis was "The Labor Policy of the American Trust." His first summer vacation after our return to Berkeley, he went on to Wisconsin, chiefly to see Commons, and then to Chicago, to study the stockyards at first-hand, and the steel industry. He wrote: "Have just seen Commons, who was *fine*. He said: 'Send me as soon as possible the outline of your thesis and I will pass upon it according to my lights.' . . . He is very interested in one of my principal subdivisions, i.e. 'Technique and Unionism,' or 'Technique and Labor.' Believes it is a big new consideration." Again he wrote: "I have just finished working through a book on 'Immigration' by Professor Fairchild of Yale, — 437 pages published three weeks ago, — lent me by Professor Ross. It is the very book I have been looking for and is *superb*. I can't get over how stimulating this looking in on a group of University men has been. It in itself is worth the trip. I feel sure of my field of work; that I am not going off in unfruitful directions; that I am keeping up with the wagon. I am now set on finishing my book right away — want it out within a year from December." From Chicago he wrote: "Am here with the reek of the stockyards in my nose, and just four blocks from them. Here lived, in this house, Upton Sinclair when he wrote 'The Jungle.'" And Mary McDowell, at the University Settlement where he was staying, told a friend of ours since Carl's death about how he came to the table that first night and no one paid much attention to him — just some young Westerner nosing about. But by the end of the meal he had the whole group leaning elbows on the table, listening to everything he had to say; and she added, "Every one of us loved him from then on."

He wrote, after visiting Swift's plant, of "seeing illustrations for all the lectures on technique I have given, and Gee! it felt good. [I could not quote him honestly and leave out his "gees"] to actually look at things being done the way one has orated about 'em being done. The thing for me to do here is to see, and see the things I'm going to write into my thesis. I want to spend a week, if I can, digging into the steel industry. With my fine information about the ore [he had just acquired that], I am anxious to fill out my knowledge of the operation of smelting and making steel. Then I can orate industrial dope." Later: "This morning I called on the Vice-President of the Illinois Steel Company, on the Treasurer of Armour & Co., and lunched with Mr. Crane of Crane Co. — Ahem!"

The time we had when it came to the actual printing of the thesis! It had to be finished by a certain day, in order to make a certain steamer, to reach Heidelberg when promised. I got in a corner of a printing-office and read proof just as fast as it came off the press, while Carl worked at home, under you can guess what pressure, to complete his manuscript — tearing down with new batches for me to get in shape for the type-setter, and then racing home to do more writing. We finished the thesis about one o'clock one morning, proof-reading and all; and the next day — or that same day, later — war was declared. Which meant just this — that the University of Heidelberg sent word that it would not be safe for Carl to send over his thesis, — there were about three or four hundred copies to go, according to German University regulations, — until the situation had quieted down somewhat. The result was that those three or four hundred copies lay stacked up in the printing-office for three or four years, until at last Carl decided it was not a very good thesis anyway, and he did n't want any one to see it, and he would write another brand-new one when peace was declared and it could get safely to its destination. So he told the printer-man to do away with the whole batch. This meant that we were out about a hundred and fifty dollars, oh, luckless thought! — a small fortune to the young Parkers. So though in a way the thesis as it stands was not meant for publication, I shall risk quoting from Part One, "The Problem," so that at least his general approach can be gathered. Remember, the title was "The Labor Policy of the American Trust."

"When the most astute critic of American labor conditions has said, 'While immigration continues in great volume, class lines will be forming and reforming, weak and instable. To prohibit or greatly restrict immigration would bring forth class conflict within a generation,' what does it mean?

"President Woodrow Wilson in a statement of his fundamental beliefs has said: 'Why are we in the presence, why are we at the threshold, of a revolution? . . . Don't you know that some man with eloquent tongue, without conscience, who did not care for the nation, could put this whole country into a flame? Don't you know that this country, from one end to the other, believes that something is wrong? What an opportunity it would be for some man without conscience to spring up and say: "This is the way; follow me" — and lead in paths of destruction!' What does it mean?

"The problem of the social unrest must seek for its source in all three classes of society! Two classes are employer and employee, the third is the great middle class, looking on. What is the relationship between the dominating employing figure in American industrial life and the men who work?

"A nation-wide antagonism to trade-unions, to the idea of collective bargaining between men and employer, cannot spring from a temperamental aversion of a mere individual, however powerful, be he Carnegie, Parry, or Post, or from the common opinion in a group such as the so-called Beef Trust, or the directorate of the United States Steel Corporation. Such a hostility, characterizing as it does one of the vitally important relationships in industrial production, must seek its reason-to-be in economic causes. Profits, market, financing, are placed in certain jeopardy by such a labor policy, and this risk is not continued, generation after generation, as a casual indulgence in temper. Deep below the strong charges against the unions of narrow self-interest and un-

American limitation of output, dressed by the Citizens' Alliance in the language of the Declaration of Independence, lies a quiet economic reason for the hostility. Just as slavery was about to go because it did not pay, and America stopped building a merchant marine because it was cheaper to hire England to transport American goods, so the American Trust, as soon as it had power, abolished the American trade-union because it found it costly. What then are these economic causes which account for the hostility?

"What did the union stand in the way of? What conditions did the trust desire to establish with which the union would interfere? Or did a labor condition arise which allowed the employer to wreck the union with such ease, that he turned aside for a moment to do it, to commit an act desirable only if its performance cost little danger or money?

"The answer can be found only after an analysis of certain factors in industrial production. These are three: —

"(*a*) The control of industrial production. Not only, in whose hands has industrial capitalism for the moment fallen, but in what direction does the evolution of control tend?

"(*b*) The technique of industrial production. Technique, at times, instead of being a servant, determines by its own characteristics the character of the labor and the geographical location of the industry, and even destroys the danger of competition, if the machinery demanded by it asks for a bigger capital investment than a raiding competitor will risk.

"(c) The labor market. The labor market can be stationary as in England, can diminish as in Ireland, or increase as in New England.

"If the character of these three factors be studied, trust hostility to American labor-unions can be explained in terms of economic measure. One national characteristic, however, must be taken for granted. That is the commercialized business morality which guides American economic life. The responsibility for the moral or social effect of an act is so rarely a consideration in a decision, that it can be here neglected without error. It is not a factor."

At the close of his investigation, he took his first vacation in five years — a canoe-trip up the Brulé with Hal Bradley. That was one of our dreams that could never come true — a canoe-trip together. We almost bought the canoe at the Exposition — we looked holes through the one we wanted. Our trip was planned to the remotest detail. We never did come into our own in the matter of our vacations, although no two people could have more fun in the woods than we. But the combination of small children and no money and new babies and work — We figured that in three more years we could be sure of at least one wonderful trip a year. Anyway, we had the joy of our plannings.

CHAPTER IX

THE second term in California had just got well under way when Carl was offered the position of Executive Secretary in the State Immigration and Housing Commission of California. I remember so well the night he came home about midnight and told me. I am afraid the financial end would have determined us, even if the work itself had small appeal — which, however, was not the case. The salary offered was $4000. We were getting $1500 at the University. We were $2000 in debt from our European trip, and saw no earthly chance of ever paying it out of our University salary. We figured that we could be square with the world in one year on a $4000 salary, and then need never be swayed by financial considerations again. So Carl accepted the new job. It was the wise thing to do anyway, as matters turned out. It threw him into direct contact for the first time with the migratory laborer and the I.W.W. It gave him his first bent in the direction of labor-psychology, which was to become his intellectual passion, and he was fired with a zeal that never left him, to see that there should be less unhappiness and inequality in the world.

The concrete result of Carl's work with the Immigration Commission was the clean-up of labor camps all over California. From unsanitary, fly-ridden, dirty makeshifts were developed ordered sanitary housing accommodations, designed and executed by experts in their fields. Also he awakened, through countless talks up and down the State, some understanding of the I.W.W. and his problem; although, judging from the newspapers nowadays, his work would seem to have been almost forgotten. As the phrase went, "Carleton Parker put the migratory on the map."

I think of the Wheatland Hop-Fields riot, or the Ford and Suhr case, which Carl was appointed to investigate for the Federal government, as the dramatic incident which focused his attention on the need of a deeper approach to a sound understanding of labor and its problems, and which, in turn, justified Mr. Bruère in stating in the "New Republic": "Parker was the first of our Economists, not only to analyse the psychology of labor and especially of casual labor, but also to make his analysis the basis for an applied technique of industrial and social reconstruction." Also, that was the occasion of his concrete introduction to the I.W.W. He wrote an account of it, later, for the "Survey," and an article on "The California Casual and His Revolt" for the "Quarterly Journal of Economics," in November, 1915.

It is all interesting enough, I feel, to warrant going into some detail.

The setting of the riot is best given in the article above referred to, "The California Casual and His Revolt."

"The story of the Wheatland hop-pickers' riot is as simple as the facts of it are new and naïve in strike histories. Twenty-eight hundred pickers were camped on a treeless hill which was part of the ——— ranch, the largest single employer of agricultural labor in the state. Some were in tents, some in topless squares of sacking, or with piles of straw. There was no organization for sanitation, no garbage-disposal. The temperature during the week of the riot had remained near 105°, and though the wells were a mile from where the men, women, and children were picking, and their bags could not be left for fear of theft of the hops, no water was sent into the fields. A lemonade wagon appeared at the end of the week, later found to be a concession granted to a cousin of the ranch owner. Local Wheatland stores were forbidden to send delivery wagons to the camp grounds. It developed in the state investigation that the owner of the ranch received half of the net profits earned by an alleged independent grocery store, which had been granted the 'grocery concession' and was located in the centre of the camp ground. . . .

"The pickers began coming to Wheatland on Tuesday, and by Sunday the irritation over the wage-scale, the absence of water in the fields, plus the persistent heat and the increasing indignity of the camp, had resulted in mass meetings, violent talk, and a general strike.

"The ranch owner, a nervous man, was harassed by the rush of work brought on by the too rapidly ripening hops, and indignant at the jeers and catcalls which greeted his appearance near the meetings of the pickers. Confused with a crisis outside his slender social philosophy, he acted true to his tradition, and perhaps his type, and called on a sheriff's posse. What industrial relationship had existed was too insecure to stand such a procedure. It disappeared entirely, leaving in control the instincts and vagaries of a mob on the one hand, and great apprehension and inexperience on the other.

"As if a stage had been set, the posse arrived in automobiles at the instant when the officially 'wanted' strike-leader was addressing a mass meeting of excited men, women, and children. After a short and typical period of skirmishing and the minor and major events of arresting a person under such circumstances, a member of the posse standing outside fired a double-barreled shot-gun over the heads of the crowd, 'to sober them,' as he explained it. Four men were killed — two of the posse and two strikers; the posse fled in their automobiles to the county seat, and all that night the roads out of Wheatland were filled with pickers leaving the camp. Eight months later, two hop-pickers, proved to be the leaders of the strike and its agitation, were convicted of murder in the first degree and sentenced to life imprisonment. Their appeal for a new trial was denied."

In his report to the Governor, written in 1914, Carl characterized the case as follows: —

"The occurrence known as the Wheatland Hop-Fields riot took place on Sunday afternoon, August 3, 1913. Growing discontent among the hop-pickers over wages, neglected camp-sanitation and absence of water in the fields had resulted in spasmodic meetings of protest on Saturday and Sunday morning, and finally by Sunday noon in a more or less involuntary strike. At five o'clock on Sunday about one thousand pickers gathered about a dance pavilion to listen to speakers. Two automobiles carrying a sheriff's posse drove up to this meeting, and officials armed with guns and revolvers attempted to disperse the crowd and to arrest, on a John Doe warrant, Richard Ford, the apparent leader of the strike. In the ensuing confusion shooting began and some twenty shots were fired. Two pickers, a deputy sheriff, and the district attorney of the county were killed. The posse fled and the camp remained unpoliced until the State Militia arrived at dawn next morning.

"The occurrence has grown from a casual, though bloody, event in California labor history into such a focus for discussion and analysis of the State's great migratory labor-problem that the incident can well be said to begin, for the commonwealth, a new and momentous labor epoch.

"The problem of vagrancy; that of the unemployed and the unemployable; the vexing conflict between the right of agitation and free speech and the law relating to criminal conspiracy; the housing and wages of agricultural laborers; the efficiency and sense of responsibility found in a posse of country deputies; the temper of the country people faced with the confusion and rioting of a labor outbreak; all these problems have found a starting point for their new and vigorous analysis in the Wheatland riot.

In the same report, submitted a year before the "Quarterly Journal" article, and almost a year before his study of psychology began, Carl wrote: —

"The manager and part-owner of the ranch is an example of a certain type of California employer. The refusal of this type to meet the social responsibilities which come with the hiring of human beings for labor, not only works concrete and cruelly unnecessary misery upon a class little able to combat personal indignity and degradation, but adds fuel to the fire of resentment and unrest which is beginning to burn in the uncared-for migratory worker in California. That —— could refuse his clear duty of real trusteeship of a camp on his own ranch, which contained hundreds of women and children, is a social fact of miserable import. The excuses we have heard of unpreparedness, of alleged ignorance of conditions, are shamed by the proven human suffering and humiliation repeated each day of the week, from Wednesday to Sunday. Even where the employer's innate sense of moral obligation fails to point out his duty, he should have realized the insanity of stimulating unrest and bitterness in this inflammable labor force. The riot on the —— ranch is a California contribution to the literature of the social unrest in America."

As to the "Legal and Economic Aspects" of the case, again quoting from the report to the Governor:—

"The position taken by the defense and their sympathizers in the course of the trial has not only an economic and social bearing, but many arguments made before the court are distinct efforts to introduce sociological modifications of the law which will have a far-reaching effect on the industrial relations of capital and labor. It is asserted that the common law,

on which American jurisprudence is founded, is known
as an ever-developing law, which must adapt itself
to changing economic and social conditions; and, in
this connection, it is claimed that the established theories of legal causation must be enlarged to include
economic and social factors in the chain of causes
leading to a result. Concretely, it is argued: —

"First, That, when unsanitary conditions lead to
discontent so intense that the crowd can be incited
to bloodshed, those responsible for the unsanitary
conditions are to be held legally responsible for the
bloodshed, as well as the actual inciters of the riot.

"Second, That, if the law will not reach out so far
as to hold the creator of unsanitary, unlivable conditions guilty of bloodshed, at any rate such conditions
excuse the inciters from liability, because inciters are
the involuntary transmitting agents of an uncon-
trollable force set in motion by those who created the
unlivable conditions. . . .

"Furthermore, on the legal side, modifications of
the law of property are urged. It is argued that modern law no longer holds the rights of private property
sacred, that these rights are being constantly regu-
lated and limited, and that in the Wheatland case the
owner's traditional rights in relation to his own lands
are to be held subject to the right of the laborers to
organize thereon. It is urged that a worker on land
has a 'property right in his job,' and that he cannot
be made to leave the job, or the land, merely because
he is trying to organize his fellow workers to make
a protest as to living and economic conditions. It is

urged that the organizing worker cannot be made to leave the job because the job is *his* property and it is all that he has."

As to "The Remedy": —

"It is obvious that the violent strike methods adopted by the I.W.W. type agitators, which only incidentally, although effectively, tend to improve camp conditions, are not to be accepted as a solution of the problem. It is also obvious that the conviction of the agitators, such as Ford and Suhr, of murder, is not a solution, but is only the punishment or revenge inflicted by organized society for a past deed. The Remedy lies in prevention.

"It is the opinion of your investigator that the improvement of living conditions in the labor camps will have the immediate effect of making the recurrence of impassioned, violent strikes and riots not only improbable, but impossible; and furthermore, such improvement will go far towards eradicating the hatred and bitterness in the minds of the employers and in the minds of the roving, migratory laborers. This accomplished, the two conflicting parties will be in a position to meet on a saner, more constructive basis, in solving the further industrial problems arising between them. . . .

"They must come to realize that their own laxity in allowing the existence of unsanitary and filthy conditions gives a much-desired foothold to the very agitators of the revolutionary I.W.W. doctrines whom they so dread; they must learn that unbearable, aggravating living conditions inoculate the minds of

the otherwise peaceful workers with the germs of
bitterness and violence, as so well exemplified at the
Wheatland riot, giving the agitators a fruitful field
wherein to sow the seeds of revolt and preach the
doctrine of direct action and sabotage.

"On the other hand, the migratory laborers must
be shown that revolts accompanied by force in scattered and isolated localities not only involve serious
breaches of law and lead to crime, but that they
accomplish no lasting constructive results in advanc-
ing their cause.

"The Commission intends to furnish a clearing-
house to hear complaints of grievances, of both sides,
and act as a mediator or safety-valve."

In the report to the Governor appear Carl's first
writings on the I.W.W.

"Of this entire labor force at the —— ranch, it
appears that some 100 had been I.W.W. 'card men,'
or had had affiliations with that organization. There
is evidence that there was in this camp a loosely
caught together camp local of the I.W.W., with about
30 active members. It is suggestive that these 30 men,
through a spasmodic action, and with the aid of the
deplorable camp conditions, dominated a heterogeneous mass of 2800 unskilled laborers in 3 days. Some
700 or 800 of the force were of the 'hobo' class, in
every sense potential I.W.W. strikers. At least 400
knew in a rough way the — for them curiously attrac-
tive — philosophy of the I.W.W., and could also sing
some of its songs.

"Of the 100-odd 'card men' of the I.W.W., some

had been through the San Diego affair, some had been
soap-boxers in Fresno, a dozen had been in the Free
Speech fight in Spokane. They sized up the hop-field
as a ripe opportunity, as the principal defendant,
'Blackie' Ford, puts it, 'to start something.' On
Friday, two days after picking began, the practical
agitators began working through the camp. Whether
or not Ford came to the ——— ranch to foment trouble
seems immaterial. There are five Fords in every
camp of seasonal laborers in California. We have
devoted ourselves in these weeks to such questions
as this: 'How big a per cent of California's migratory
seasonal labor force know the technique of an I.W.W.
strike?' 'How many of the migratory laborers know
when conditions are ripe to "start something"?' We
are convinced that among the individuals of every
fruit-farm labor group are many potential strikers.
Where a group of hoboes sit around a fire under a
railroad bridge, many of the group can sing I.W.W.
songs without the book. This was not so three years
ago. The I.W.W. in California is not a closely organized body, with a steady membership. The rank and
file know little of the technical organization of industrial life which their written constitution demands.
They listen eagerly to the appeal for the 'solidarity'
of their class. In the dignifying of vagabondage
through their crude but virile song and verse, in the
bitter vilification of the jail turnkey and county
sheriff, in their condemnation of the church and its
formal social work, they find the vindication of their
hobo status which they desire. They cannot sustain

a live organization unless they have a strike or free-speech fight to stimulate their spirit. It is in their methods of warfare, not in their abstract philosophy or even hatred of law and judges, that danger lies for organized society. Since every one of the 5000 laborers in California who have been at some time connected with the I.W.W. considers himself a 'camp delegate' with walking papers to organize a camp local, this small army is watching, as Ford did, for an unsanitary camp or low wage-scale, to start the strike which will not only create a new I.W.W. local, but bring fame to the organizer. This common acceptance of direct action and sabotage as the rule of operation, the songs and the common vocabulary are, we feel convinced, the first stirring of a class expression.

"Class solidarity they have not. That may never come, for the migratory laborer has neither the force nor the vision nor tenacity to hold long enough to the ideal to attain it. But the I.W.W. is teaching a method of action which will give this class in violent flare-ups, such as that at Wheatland, expression.

"The dying away of the organization after the outburst is, therefore, to be expected. Their social condition is a miserable one. Their work, even at the best, must be irregular. They have nothing to lose in a strike, and, as a leader put it, 'A riot and a chance to blackguard a jailer is about the only intellectual fun we have.'

"Taking into consideration the misery and physical privation and the barren outlook of this life of the seasonal worker, the I.W.W. movement, with all its irresponsible motive and unlawful action, becomes in reality a class-protest, and the dignity which this characteristic gives it perhaps alone explains the persistence of the organization in the field.

"Those attending the protest mass-meeting of the Wheatland hop-pickers were singing the I.W.W. song 'Mr. Block,' when the sheriff's posse came up in its automobiles. The crowd had been harangued by an experienced I.W.W. orator — 'Blackie' Ford. They had been told, according to evidence, to 'knock the blocks off the scissor-bills.' Ford had taken a sick baby from its mother's arms and, holding it before the eyes of the 1500 people, had cried out: 'It's for the life of the kids we're doing this.' Not a quarter of the crowd was of a type normally venturesome enough to strike, and yet, when the sheriff went after Ford, he was knocked down and kicked senseless by infuriated men. In the bloody riot which then ensued, District Attorney Manwell, Deputy Sheriff Riordan, a negro Porto Rican and the English boy were shot and killed. Many were wounded. The posse literally fled, and the camp remained practically unpoliced until the State Militia arrived at dawn the next day.

"The question of social responsibility is one of the deepest significance. The posse was, I am convinced, over-nervous and, unfortunately, over-rigorous. This can be explained in part by the state-wide apprehension over the I.W.W.; in part by the normal California country posse's attitude toward a labor trouble. A deputy sheriff, at the most critical moment, fired a shot in the air, as he stated, 'to sober the crowd.'

There were armed men in the crowd, for every crowd
of 2000 casual laborers includes a score of gunmen.
Evidence goes to show that even the gentler moun-
tainfolk in the crowd had been aroused to a sense of
personal injury. ——'s automobile had brought part
of the posse. Numberless pickers cling to the belief
that the posse was '——'s police.' When Deputy
Sheriff Dakin shot into the air, a fusillade took place;
and when he had fired his last shell, an infuriated
crowd of men and women chased him to the ranch
store, where he was forced to barricade himself. The
crowd was dangerous and struck the first blow. The
murderous temper which turned the crowd into a mob
is incompatible with social existence, let alone social
progress. The crowd at the moment of the shooting
was a wild and lawless animal. But to your investigator the important subject to analyze is not the guilt
or innocence of Ford or Suhr, as the direct stimulators
of the mob in action, but to name and standardize the
early and equally important contributors to a psychological situation which resulted in an unlawful killing.
If this is done, how can we omit either the filth of the
hop-ranch, the cheap gun-talk of the ordinary deputy
sheriff, or the unbridled, irresponsible speech of the
soap-box orator?

"Without doubt the propaganda which the I.W.W.
had actually adopted for the California seasonal
worker can be, in its fairly normal working out in law,
a criminal conspiracy, and under that charge, Ford
and Suhr have been found guilty of the Wheatland
murder. But the important fact is, that this propa-

ganda will be carried out, whether unlawful or not.
We have talked hours with the I.W.W. leaders, and
they are absolutely conscious of their position in the
eyes of the law. Their only comment is that they are
glad, if it must be a conspiracy, that it is a criminal
conspiracy. They have volunteered the beginning of
a cure; it is to clean up the housing and wage problem
of the seasonal worker. The shrewdest I.W.W. leader
we found said: 'We can't agitate in the country unless things are rotten enough to bring the crowd along.'
They evidently were in Wheatland."

He was high ace with the Wobbly for a while. They
invited him to their Jungles, they carved him presents in jail. I remember a talk he gave on some phase
of the California labor-problem one Sunday night, at
the Congregational church in Oakland. The last three
rows were filled with unshaven hoboes, who filed up
afterwards, to the evident distress of the clean regular
church-goers, to clasp his hand. They withdrew their
allegiance after a time, which naturally in no way
phased Carl's scientific interest in them. A paper hostile to Carl's attitude on the I.W.W. and his insistence
on the clean-up of camps published an article por-
traying him as a double-faced individual who feigned
an interest in the under-dog really to undo him, as he
was at heart and pocket-book a capitalist, being the
possessor of an independent income of $150,000 a
year. Some I.W.W.'s took this up, and convinced a
large meeting that he was really trying to sell them
out. It is not only the rich who are fickle. Some of
them remained his firm friends always, however.

That summer two of his students hoboed it till they came down with malaria, in the meantime turning in a fund of invaluable facts regarding the migratory and his life.

A year later, in his article in the "Quarterly Journal," and, be it remembered, after his study of psychology had begun, Carl wrote: —

"There is here, beyond a doubt, a great laboring population experiencing a high suppression of normal instincts and traditions. There can be no greater perversion of a desirable existence than this insecure, under-nourished, wandering life, with its sordid sex-expression and reckless and rare pleasures. Such a life leads to one of two consequences: either a sinking of the class to a low and hopeless level, where they become, through irresponsible conduct and economic inefficiency, a charge upon society; or revolt and guerrilla labor warfare.

"The migratory laborers, as a class, are the finished product of an environment which seems cruelly efficient in turning out beings moulded after all the standards society abhors. Fortunately the psychologists have made it unnecessary to explain that there is nothing willful or personally reprehensible in the vagrancy of these vagrants. Their histories show that, starting with the long hours and dreary winters of the farms they ran away from, through their character-debasing experience with irregular industrial labor, on to the vicious economic life of the winter unemployed, their training predetermined but one outcome. Nurture has triumphed over nature; the environment has produced its type. Difficult though the organization of these people may be, a coincidence of favoring conditions may place an opportunity in the hands of a super-leader. If this comes, one can be sure that California will be both very astonished and very misused."

I was told only recently of a Belgian economics professor, out here in California during the war, on official business connected with aviation. He asked at once to see Carl, but was told we had moved to Seattle. "My colleagues in Belgium asked me to be sure and see Professor Parker," he said, "as we consider him the one man in America who understands the problem of the migratory laborer."

That winter Carl got the city of San José to stand behind a model unemployed lodging-house, one of the two students who had "hoboed" during the summer taking charge of it. The unemployed problem, as he ran into it at every turn, stirred Carl to his depths. At one time he felt it so strongly that he wanted to start a lodging-house in Berkeley, himself, just to be helping out somehow, even though it would be only surface help.

It was also about this time that California was treated to the spectacle of an Unemployed Army, which was driven from pillar to post, — or, in this case, from town to town, — each trying to outdo the last in protestations of unhospitality. Finally, in Sacramento the fire-hoses were turned on the army. At that Carl flamed with indignation, and expressed himself in no mincing terms, both to the public and to the reporter who sought his views. He was no hand to keep clippings, but I did come across one of his milder interviews in the San Francisco "Bulletin" of March 11, 1914.

"That California's method of handling the unemployed problem is in accord with the 'careless, cruel and unscientific attitude of society on the labor question,' is the statement made to-day by Professor Carleton H. Parker, Assistant Professor of Industrial economy, and secretary of the State Immigration Committee.

"'There are two ways of looking at this winter's unemployed problem,' said Dr. Parker; 'one is fatally bad and the other promises good. One way is shallow and biased; the other strives to use the simple rules of science for the analysis of any problem. One way is to damn the army of the unemployed and the irresponsible, irritating vagrants who will not work. The other way is to admit that any such social phenomenon as this army is just as normal a product of our social organization as our own university.

"'Much street-car and ferry analysis of this problem that I have overheard seems to believe that this army created its own degraded self, that a vagrant is a vagrant from personal desire and perversion. This analysis is as shallow as it is untrue. If unemployment and vagrancy are the product of our careless, indifferent society over the half-century, then its cure will come only by a half-century's careful regretful social labor by this same tardy society.

"'The riot at Sacramento is merely the appearance

of the problem from the back streets into the strong light. The handling of the problem there is unhappily in accord with the careless, cruel attitude of society on this question. We are willing to respect the anxiety of Sacramento, threatened in the night with this irresponsible, reckless invasion; but how can the city demand of vagrants observance of the law, when they drop into mob-assertion the minute the problem comes up to them?'"

The illustration he always used to express his opinion of the average solution of unemployment, I quote from a paper of his on that subject, written in the spring of 1915.

"There is an old test for insanity which is made as follows: the suspect is given a cup, and is told to empty a bucket into which water is running from a faucet. If the suspect turns off the water before he begins to bail out the bucket, he is sane. Nearly all the current solutions of unemployment leave the faucet running. . . .

"The heart of the problem, the cause, one might well say, of unemployment, is that the employment of men regularly or irregularly is at no time an important consideration of those minds which control industry. Social organization has ordered it that these minds shall be interested only in achieving a reasonable profit in the manufacture and the sale of goods. Society has never demanded that industries be run even in part to give men employment. Rewards are not held out for such a policy, and therefore it is unreasonable to expect such a performance. Though a favorite popular belief is that we must 'work to live,' we have no current adage of a 'right to work.' This winter there are shoeless men and women, closed shoe-factories, and destitute shoemakers; children in New England with no woolen clothing, half-time woolen mills, and unemployed spinners and weavers. Why? Simply because the mills cannot turn out the reasonable business profit; and since that is the only promise that can galvanize them into activity, they stand idle, no matter how much humanity finds of misery and death in this decision. This statement is not a peroration to a declaration for Socialism. It seems a fair rendering of the matter-of-fact logic of the analysis.

"It seems hopeless, and also unfair, to expect out-of-work insurance, employment bureaus, or philanthropy, to counteract the controlling force of profit-seeking. There is every reason to believe that profit-seeking has been a tremendous stimulus to economic activity in the past. It is doubtful if the present great accumulation of capital would have come into existence without it. But to-day it seems as it were to be caught up by its own social consequences. It is hard to escape from the insistence of a situation in which the money a workman makes in a year fails to cover the upkeep of his family; and this impairment of the father's income through unemployment has largely to be met by child- and woman-labor. The Federal Immigration Commission's report shows that in not a single great American industry can the average yearly income of the father keep his family. Seven hundred and fifty dollars is the bare minimum for the maintenance of the average-sized American industrial family. The average yearly earnings of the heads of families working in the United States in the iron and steel industry is $409; in bituminous coal-mining $451; in the woolen industry $400; in silk $448; in cotton $470; in clothing $530; in boots and shoes $573; in leather $511; in sugar-refining $549; in the meat industry $578; in furniture $598, etc.

"He who decries created work, municipal lodging-houses, bread-lines, or even sentimental charity, in the face of the winter's destitution, has an unsocial soul. The most despicable thing to-day is the whine of our cities lest their inadequate catering to their own home-less draw a few vagrants from afar. But when the agony of our winter makeshifting is by, will a sufficient minority of our citizens rise and demand that the best technical, economic, and sociological brains in our wealthy nation devote themselves with all courage and honesty to the problem of unemployment?"

Carl was no diplomat, in any sense of the word — above all, no political diplomat. It is a wonder that the Immigration and Housing Commission stood behind him as long as it did. He grew rabid at every political appointment which, in his eyes, hampered his work. It was evident, so they felt, that he was not tactful in his relations with various members of the Commission. It all galled him terribly, and after much consultation at home, he handed in his resignation. During the first term of his secretaryship, from October to December, he carried his full-time University work. From January to May he had a seminar only, as I remember. From August on he gave no University work at all; so, after asking to have his resignation from the Commission take effect at once, he had at once to find something to do to support his family.

This was in October, 1914, after just one year as Executive Secretary. We were over in Contra Costa County then, on a little ranch of my father's. Berkeley socially had come to be too much of a strain, and, too, we wanted the blessed sons to have a real country experience. Ten months we were there. Three days after Carl resigned, he was on his way to Phœnix, Arizona, — where there was a threatened union tie-up, — as United States Government investigator of the labor situation. He added thereby to his first-hand stock of labor-knowledge, made a firm friend of Governor Hunt, — he was especially interested in his prison policy, — and in those few weeks was the richer by one more of the really intimate friendships one counts on to the last — Will Scarlett.

He wrote, on Carl's death, "What a horrible, hideous loss! Any of us could so easily have been spared; that he, who was of such value, had to go seems such an utter waste. . . . He was one of that very, very small circle of men, whom, in the course of our lives, we come *really* to love. His friendship meant so much — though I heard but infrequently from him, there was the satisfaction of a deep friendship that was *always there* and *always the same*. He would have gone so far! I have looked forward to a great career for him, and had such pride in him. It's too hideous!"

CHAPTER X

IN January, 1915, Carl took up his teaching again in real earnest, commuting to Alamo every night. I would have the boys in bed and the little supper all ready by the fire; then I would prowl down the road with my electric torch, to meet him coming home; he would signal in the distance with his torch, and I with mine. Then the walk back together, sometimes ankle-deep in mud; then supper, making the toast over the coals, and an evening absolutely to ourselves. And never in all our lives did we ask for more joy than that.

That spring we began building our very own home in Berkeley. The months in Alamo had made us feel that we could never bear to be in the centre of things again, nor, for that matter, could we afford a lot in the centre of things; so we bought high up on the Berkeley hills, where we could realize as much privacy as was possible, and yet where our friends could reach us — if they could stand the climb. The love of a nest we built! We were longer in that house than anywhere else: two years almost to the day — two years of such happiness as no other home has ever seen. There, around the redwood table in the living-room, by the window overlooking the Golden Gate, we had the suppers that meant much joy to us and I hope to the friends we gathered around us. There, on the porches overhanging the very Canyon itself we had our Sunday tea-parties. (Each time Carl would plead, "I don't have to wear a stiff collar, do I?" and he knew that I would answer, "You wear anything you want," which usually meant a blue soft shirt.)

We had a little swimming-tank in back, for the boys.

And then, most wonderful of all, came the day when the June-Bug was born, the daughter who was to be the very light of her adoring father's eyes. (Her real name is Alice Lee.) "Mother, there never really *was* such a baby, *was* there?" he would ask ten times a day. She was not born up on the hill; but in ten days we were back from the hospital and out day and night through that glorious July, on some one of the porches overlooking the bay and the hills. And we added our adored Nurse Balch as a friend of the family forever.

I always think of Nurse Balch as the person who more than any other, perhaps, understood to some degree just what happiness filled our lives day in and day out. No one assumes anything before a trained nurse — they are around too constantly for that. They see the misery in homes, they see what joy there is. And Nurse Balch saw, because she was around practically all the time for six weeks, that there was nothing but joy every minute of the day in our home. I do not know how I can make people understand, who are used to just ordinary happiness, what sort of a life Carl and I led. It was not just that we got along. It was an active, not a passive state. There was never a home-coming, say at lunch-time, that did not seem an event — when our curve of happiness abruptly rose. Meals were joyous occasions always; perhaps too scant attention paid to the manners of the young, but much gurglings, and "Tell some more, daddy," and always detailed accounts of every little happening during the last few hours of separation.

Then there was ever the difficulty of good-byes, though it meant only for a few hours, until supper. And at supper-time he would come up the front stairs, I waiting for him at the top, perhaps limping. That was his little joke — we had many little family jokes. Limping meant that I was to look in every pocket until I unearthed a bag of peanut candy. Usually he was laden with bundles — provisions, shoes from the cobbler, a tennis-racket restrung, and an armful of books. After greetings, always the question, "How's my June-Bug?" and a family procession upstairs to peer over a crib at a fat gurgler. And "Mother, there never really *was* such a baby, *was* there?" No, nor such a father.

It was that first summer back in Berkeley, the year before the June-Bug was born, when Carl was teaching in Summer School, that we had our definite enthusiasm over labor-psychology aroused. Will Ogburn, who was also teaching at Summer School that year, and whose lectures I attended, introduced us to Hart's "Psychology of Insanity," several books by Freud, McDougall's "Social Psychology," etc. I remember Carl's seminar the following spring — his last seminar at the University of California. He had started with nine seminar students three years before; now there were thirty-three. They were all such a superior picked lot, some seniors, mostly graduates, that he felt there was no one he could ask to stay out. I visited it all the term, and I am sure that nowhere else on the campus could quite such heated and excited discussions have been heard — Carl simply sitting at the head of the table, directing here, leading there.

The general subject was Labor-Problems. The students had to read one book a week — such books as Hart's "Psychology of Insanity," Keller's "Societal Evolution," Holt's "Freudian Wish," McDougall's "Social Psychology," — two weeks to that, — Lippmann's "Preface to Politics," Veblen's "Instinct of Workmanship," Wallas's "Great Society," Thorndike's "Educational Psychology," Hoxie's "Scientific Management," Ware's "The Worker and his Country," G. H. Parker's "Biology and Social Problems," and so forth — and ending, as a concession to the idealists, with Royce's "Philosophy of Loyalty."

One of the graduate students of the seminar wrote me: "For three years I sat in his seminar on Labor-Problems, and had we both been there ten years longer, each season would have found me in his class. His influence on my intellectual life was by far the most stimulating and helpful of all the men I have known. . . . But his spirit and influence will live on in the lives of those who sat at his feet and learned."

The seminar was too large, really, for intimate discussion, so after a few weeks several of the boys asked Carl if they could have a little sub-seminar. It was a very rushed time for him, but he said that, if they would arrange all the details, he would save them Tuesday evenings. So every Tuesday night about a dozen boys climbed our hill to rediscuss the subject of the seminar of that afternoon — and everything else under the heavens and beyond. I laid out ham sandwiches, or sausages, or some edible dear to the male heart, and coffee to be warmed, and about midnight could be heard the sounds of banqueting from the kitchen. Three students told me on graduation that those Tuesday nights at our house had meant more intellectual stimulus than anything that ever came into their lives.

One of these boys wrote to me after Carl's death: —

"When I heard that Doc had gone, one of the finest and cleanest men I have ever had the privilege of associating with, I seemed to have stopped thinking. It did n't seem possible to me, and I can remember very clearly of thinking what a rotten world this is when we have to live and lose a man like Doc. I have talked to two men who were associated with him in somewhat the same manner as I was, and we simply looked at one another after the first sentences, and then I guess the thoughts of a man who had made so much of an impression on our minds drove coherent speech away. . . . I have had the opportunity since leaving college of experiencing something real besides college life and I can't remember during all that period of not having wondered how Dr. Parker would handle this or that situation. He was simply immense to me at all times, and if love of a man-to-man kind does exist, then I truthfully can say that I had that love for him."

Of the letters received from students of those years I should like to quote a passage here and there.

An aviator in France writes: "There was no man like him in my college life. Believe me, he has been a figure in all we do over here, — we who knew him, — and a reason for our doing, too. His loss is so great to all of us! . . . He was so fine he will always push us on to finding the truth about things. That was his great spark, was n't it?"

From a second lieutenant in France: "I loved Carl. He was far more to me than just a friend — he was father, brother, and friend all in one. He influenced, as you know, everything I have done since I knew him — for it was his enthusiasm which has been the force which determined the direction of my work. And the bottom seemed to have fallen out of my whole scheme of things when the word just came to me."

From one of the young officers at Camp Lewis: "When E—— told me about Carl's illness last Wednesday, I resolved to go and see him the coming week-end. I carried out my resolution, only to find that I could see neither him nor you. [This was the day before Carl's death.] It was a great disappointment to me, so I left some flowers and went away. . . . I simply could not leave Seattle without seeing Carl once more, so I made up my mind to go out to the undertaker's. The friends I was with discouraged the idea, but it was too strong within me. There was a void within me which could only be filled by seeing

my friend once more. I went out there and stood by
his side for quite a while. I recalled the happy days
spent with him on the campus. I thought of his kindliness, his loyalty, his devotion. Carl Parker shall
always occupy a place in the recesses of my memory
as a true example of nobility. It was hard for me to
leave, but I felt much better."

From one of his women students: "Always from
the first day when I knew him he seemed to give me
a joy of life and an inspiration to work which no other
person or thing has ever given me. And it is a joy and
an inspiration I shall always keep. I seldom come to
a stumbling-block in my work that I don't stop to
wonder what Carl Parker would do were he solving
that problem."

Another letter I have chosen to quote from was
written by a former student now in Paris: —

"We could not do without him. He meant too
much to us. . . . I come now as a young friend to put
myself by your side a moment and to try to share a
great sorrow which is mine almost as much as it is
yours. For I am sure that, after you, there were few
indeed who loved Carl as much as I.

"Oh, I am remembering a hundred things! — the
first day I found you both in the little house on Hearst
Avenue — the dinners we used to have . . . the times
I used to come on Sunday morning to find you both,
and the youngsters — the day just before I graduated
when mother and I had lunch at your house . . . and,
finally, that day I left you, and you said, both of you,
'Don't come back without seeing some of the cities

of Europe.' I'd have missed some of the cities to have come back and found you both.

"Some of him we can't keep. The quaint old gray twinkle — the quiet, half-impudent, wholly confident poise with which he defied all comers—that inexhaustible and incorrigible fund of humor — those we lose. No use to whine — we lose it; write it off, gulp, go on.

"But other things we keep, none the less. The stimulus and impetus and inspiration are not lost, and shall not be. No one has counted the youngsters he has hauled, by the scruff of the neck as often as not, out of a slough of middle-class mediocrity, and sent careering off into some welter or current of ideas and conjecture. Carl did n't know where they would end, and no more do any of the rest of us. He knew he loathed stagnation. And he stirred things and stirred people. And the end of the stirring is far from being yet known or realized."

I like, too, a story one of the Regents told me. He ran into a student from his home town and asked how his work at the University was going. The boy looked at him eagerly and said, "Mr. M——, I 've been born again! [" Born again " — those were his very words.] I entered college thinking of it as a preparation for making more money when I got out. I 've come across a man named Parker in the faculty and am taking everything he gives. Now I know I'd be selling out my life to make money the goal. I know now, too, that whatever money I do make can never be at the expense of the happiness and welfare of any other human being."

CHAPTER XI

ABOUT this time we had a friend come into our lives
who was destined to mean great things to the Parkers
— Max Rosenberg. He had heard Carl lecture once
or twice, had met him through our good friend Dr.
Brown, and a warm friendship had developed. In
the spring of 1916 we were somewhat tempted by a
call to another University — $1700 was really not a
fortune to live on, and to make both ends meet and
prepare for the June-Bug's coming, Carl had to use
every spare minute lecturing outside. It discouraged
him, for he had no time left to read and study. So
when a call came that appealed to us in several ways,
besides paying a much larger salary, we seriously
considered it. About then "Uncle Max" rang up from
San Francisco and asked Carl to see him before answering this other University, and an appointment
was made for that afternoon.

I was to be at a formal luncheon, but told Carl to
be sure to call me up the minute he left Max — we
wondered so hard what he might mean. And what he
did mean was the most wonderful idea that ever
entered a friend's head. He felt that Carl had a real
message to give the world, and that he should write
a book. He also realized that it was impossible to find
time for a book under the circumstances. Therefore
he proposed that Carl should take a year's leave of
absence and let Max finance him — not only just

finance him, but allow for a trip throughout the East
for him to get the inspiration of contact with other
men in his field; and enough withal, so that there
should be no skimping anywhere and the little family
at home should have everything they needed.

It seemed to us something too wonderful to believe.
I remember going back to that lunch-table, after Carl
had telephoned me only the broadest details, wonder-
ing if it were the same world. That Book — we had
dreamed of writing that book for so many years —
the material to be in it changed continually, but always the longing to write, and no time, no hopes of
any chance to do it. And the June-Bug coming, and
more need for money — hence more outside lectures
than ever. I have no love for the University of California when I think of that $1700. (I quote from an
article that came out in New York: "It is an astound-
ing fact which his University must explain, that he,
with his great abilities as teacher and leader, his wide
travel and experience and training, received from the
University in his last year of service there a salary of
$1700 a year! The West does not repay commercial
genius like that.") For days after Max's offer we
hardly knew we were on earth. It was so very much
the most wonderful thing that could have happened
to us. Our friends had long ago adopted the phrase
"just Parker luck," and here was an example if there
ever was one. "Parker luck" indeed it was!

This all meant, to get the fulness out of it, that
Carl must make a trip of at least four months in the
East. At first he planned to return in the middle of it

and then go back again; but somehow four months spent as we planned it out for him seemed so absolutely marvelous, — an opportunity of a lifetime, — that joy for him was greater in my soul than the dread of a separation. It was different from any other parting we had ever had. I was bound that I would not shed a single tear when I saw him off, even though it meant the longest time apart we had experienced. Three nights before he left, being a bit blue about things, for all our fine talk, we prowled down our hillside and found our way to our first Charlie Chaplin film. We laughed until we cried — we really did. So that night, seeing Carl off, we went over that Charlie Chaplin film in detail and let ourselves think and talk of nothing else. We laughed all over again, and Carl went off laughing, and I waved good-bye laughing. Bless that Charlie Chaplin film!

It would not take much imagination to realize what that trip meant to Carl — and through him to me. From the time he first felt the importance of the application of modern psychology to the study of economics, he became more and more intellectually isolated from his colleagues. They had no interest in, no sympathy for, no understanding of, what he was driving at. From May, when college closed, to October, when he left for the East, he read prodigiously. He had a mind for assimilation — he knew where to store every new piece of knowledge he acquired, and kept thereby an orderly brain. He read more than a book a week: everything he could lay hands on in psychology, anthropology, biology, philosophy, psycho-analysis — every field which he felt contributed to his own growing conviction that orthodox economics had served its day. And how he gloried in that reading! It had been years since he had been able to do anything but just keep up with his daily lectures, such was the pressure he was working under. Bless his heart, he was always coming across something that was just too good to hold in, and I would hear him come upstairs two steps at a time, bolt into the kitchen, and say: "Just listen to this!" And he would read an extract from some new-found treasure that would make him glow.

But outside of myself, — and I was only able to keep up with him by the merest skimmings, — and one or two others at most, there was no one who understood what he was driving at. As his reading and convictions grew, he waxed more and more outraged at the way Economics was handled in his own University. He saw student after student having every ounce of intellectual curiosity ground out of them by a process of economic education that would stultify a genius. Any student who continued his economic studies did so in spite of the introductory work, not because he had had one little ounce of enthusiasm aroused in his soul. Carl would walk the floor with his hands in his pockets when kindred spirits — especially students who had gone through the mill, and as seniors or graduates looked back outraged at certain courses they had had to flounder through — brought up the subject of Economics at the University of California.

Off he went then on his pilgrimage, — his Research
Magnificent, — absolutely unknown to almost every
man he hoped to see before his return. The first stop
he made was at Columbia, Missouri, to see his idol
Veblen. He quaked a bit beforehand, — had heard
Veblen might not see him, — but the second letter
from Missouri began, "Just got in after thirteen
hours with Veblen. It went wonderfully and I am
tickled to death. He O.K.s my idea entirely and said
I could not go wrong. . . . Gee, but it is some grand
experience to go up against him."

In the next letter he told of a graduate student who
came out to get his advice regarding a thesis-subject
in labor. "I told him to go to his New England home
and study the reaction of machine-industry on the
life of the town. That is a typical Veblen subject. It
scared the student to death, and Veblen chuckled
over my advice." In Wisconsin he was especially
anxious to see Guyer. Of his visit with him he wrote:
"It was a whiz of a session. He is just my meat." At
Yale he saw Keller. "He is a wonder and is going to
do a lot for me in criticism."

Then began the daily letters from New York, and
every single letter — not only from New York but
from every other place he happened to be in: Baltimore, Philadelphia, Cambridge — told of at least one
intellectual Event — with a capital E — a day. No
one ever lived who had a more stimulating experience.
Friends would ask me: "What is the news from Carl?"
And I would just gasp. Every letter was so full of the
new influences coming into his life, that it was im-

possible to give even an idea of the history in the making that was going on with the Parkers.

In the first days in New York he saw T. H. Morgan. "I just walked in on him and introduced myself baldly, and he is a corker. A remarkable talker, with a mind like a flash. I am to see him again. To-morrow will be a big day for me — I'll see Hollingworth, and very probably Thorndike, and I'll know then something of what I'll get out of New York." Next day: "Called on Hollingworth to-day. He gave me some invaluable data and opinions. . . . To-morrow I see Thorndike." And the next day: "I'm so joyful and excited over Thorndike. He was so enthusiastic over my work. . . . He at once had brass-tack ideas. Said I was right — that strikes usually started because of small and very human violations of man's innate dispositions."

Later he called on Professor W. C. Mitchell. "He went into my thesis very fully and is all for it. Professor Mitchell knows more than any one the importance of psychology to economics and he is all for my study. Gee, but I get excited after such a session. I bet I'll get out a real book, my girl!"

After one week in New York he wrote: "The trip has paid for itself now, and I'm dead eager to view the time when I begin my writing." Later: "Just got in from a six-hour session with the most important group of employers in New York. I sat in on a meeting of the Building Trades Board where labor delegates and employers appeared. After two hours of it (awfully interesting) the Board took me to dinner and we talked labor stuff till ten-thirty. Gee, it was fine, and I got oceans of stuff."

Then came Boas, and more visits with Thorndike. "To-night I put in six hours with Thorndike, and am pleased plum to death. . . . Under his friendly stimulus I developed a heap of new ideas; and say, wait till I begin writing! I 'll have ten volumes at the present rate. . . . This visit with Thorndike was worth the whole trip." (And in turn Thorndike wrote me: "The days that he and I spent together in New York talking of these things are one of my finest memories and I appreciate the chance that let me meet him.") He wrote from the Harvard Club, where Walter Lippmann put him up: "The Dad is a 'prominent clubman.' Just lolled back at lunch, in a room with animals (stuffed) all around the walls, and waiters flying about, and a ceiling up a mile. Gee!" Later: "I just had a most wonderful visit with the Director of the National Committee for Mental Hygiene, Dr. Solman, and he is a wiz, a wiz!"

Next day: "Had a remarkable visit with Dr. Gregory this A.M. He is one of the greatest psychiatrists in New York and up on balkings, business tension, and the mental effect of monotonous work. He was so worked up over my explanation of unrest (a mental status) through instinct-balkings other than sex, that he asked if I would consider using his big psychopathic ward as a laboratory field for my own work. Then he dated me up for a luncheon at which three of the biggest mental specialists in New York will be present, to talk over the manner in which psychiatry will aid my research! I can't say how tickled I am over his attitude." Next letter: "At ten reached Dr. Pierce Bailey's, the big psychiatrist, and for an hour and a half we talked, and I was simply tickled to death. He is really a wonder and I was very enthused. . . . Before leaving he said: 'You come to dinner Friday night here and I will have Dr. Paton from Princeton and I'll get in some more to meet you.' . . . Then I beat it to the 'New Republic' offices, and sat down to dinner with the staff plus Robert Bruère, and the subject became 'What is a labor policy?' The Dad, he did his share, he did, and had a great row with Walter Lippmann and Bruère. Walter Lippmann said: 'This won't do — you have made me doubt a lot of things. You come to lunch with me Friday at the Harvard Club and we'll thrash it all out.' Says I, 'All right!' Then says Croly, 'This won't do; we'll have a dinner here the following Monday night, and I'll get Felix Frankfurter down from Boston, and we'll thrash it out some more!' Says I, 'All right!' And says Mr. Croly, private, 'You come to dinner with us on Sunday!' — 'All right,' sez Dad. Dr. Gregory has me with Dr. Solman on Monday, and Harry Overstreet on Wednesday, Thorndike on Saturday, and gee, but I'll beat it for New Haven on Thursday, or I'll die of up-torn brain."

Are you realizing what this all meant to my Carl — until recently reading and pegging away unencouraged in his basement study up on the Berkeley hills?

The next day he heard Roosevelt at the Ritz-Carlton. "Then I watched that remarkable man wind the crowd almost around his finger. It was great, and pure psychology; and say, fool women and some fool men; but T.R. went on blithely as if every one was an intellectual giant." That night a dinner with Winston Churchill. Next letter: "Had a simply superb talk with Hollingworth for two and a half hours this afternoon. . . . The dinner was the four biggest psychiatrists in New York and Dad. Made me simply yell, it did. . . . It was for my book simply superb. All is going so wonderfully." Next day: "Now about the Thorndike dinner: it was grand. . . . I can't tell you how much these talks are maturing my ideas about the book. I think in a different plane and am certain that my ideas are surer. There have come up a lot of odd problems touching the conflict, so-called, between intelligence and instinct, and these I'm getting thrashed out grandly." After the second "New Republic" dinner he wrote: "Lots of important people there . . . Felix Frankfurter, two judges, and the two Goldmarks, Pierce Bailey, etc., and the whole staff. . . . Had been all day with Dr. Gregory and other psychiatrists and had met Police Commissioner Woods . . . a wonderfully rich day. . . . I must run for a date with Professor Robinson and then to meet Howe, the Immigration Commissioner."

Then a trip to Ellis Island, and at midnight that same date he wrote: "Just had a most truly remarkable — eight-thirty to twelve — visit with Professor Robinson, he who wrote that European history we bought in Germany." Then a trip to Philadelphia, being dined and entertained by various members of the Wharton School faculty. Then the Yale-Harvard game, followed by three days and two nights in the psychopathic ward at Sing Sing. "I found in the psychiatrist at the prison a true wonder — Dr. Glueck. He has a viewpoint on instincts which differs from any one that I have met." The next day, back in New York: "Just had a most remarkable visit with Thomas Mott Osborne." Later in the same day: "Just had an absolutely grand visit and lunch with Walter Lippmann . . . it was about the best talk with regard to my book that I have had in the East. He is an intellectual wonder and a big, good-looking, friendly boy. I'm for him a million."

Then his visit with John Dewey. "I put up to him my regular questions — the main one being the importance of the conflict between MacDougall and the Freudians. . . . He was cordiality itself. I am expecting red-letter days with him. My knowledge of the subject is increasing fast." Then a visit with Irving Fisher at New Haven. The next night "was simply remarkable." Irving Fisher took him to a banquet in New York, in honor of some French dignitaries, with President Wilson present — "at seven dollars a plate!" As to President Wilson, "He was simply great — almost the greatest, in fact is the greatest, speaker I have ever heard."

Then a run down to Cambridge, every day crammed to the edges. "Had breakfast with Felix Frankfurter. He has the grand spirit and does so finely appreciate what my subject means. He walked me down to see a friend of his, Laski, intellectually a sort of marvel

— knows psychology and philosophy cold — grand talk. Then I called on Professor Gay and he dated me for a dinner to-morrow night. Luncheon given to me by Professor Taussig — that was *fine*. . . . Then I flew to see E. B. Holt for an hour [his second visit there]. Had a grand visit, and then at six was taken with Gay to dinner with the visiting Deans at the Boston Harvard Club." (Mr. Holt wrote: "I met Mr. Parker briefly in the winter of 1916–17, briefly, but so very delightfully! I felt that he was an ally and a brilliant one.")

I give these many details because you must appreciate what this new wonder-world meant to a man who was considered nobody much by his own University.

Then one day a mere card: "This is honestly a day in which no two minutes of free time exist — so superbly grand has it gone and so fruitful for the book — the best of all yet. One of the biggest men in the United States (Cannon of Harvard) asked me to arrange my thesis to be analyzed by a group of experts in the field." Next day he wrote: "Up at six-forty-five, and at seven-thirty I was at Professor Cannon's. I put my thesis up to him strong and got one of the most encouraging and stimulating receptions I have had. He took me in to meet his wife, and said: 'This young man has stimulated and aroused me greatly. We must get his thesis formally before a group.'" Later, from New York: "From seven-thirty to eleven-thirty I argued with Dr. A. A. Brill, who translated all of Freud!!! and it was simply wonderful. I came home at twelve and wrote up a lot."

Later he went to Washington with Walter Lippmann. They ran into Colonel House on the train, and
talked foreign relations for two and a half hours. "My
hair stood on end at the importance of what he said."
From Washington he wrote: "Am having one of the
Great Experiences of my young life." Hurried full
days in Philadelphia, with a most successful talk
before the University of Pennsylvania Political and
Social Science Conference ("Successful," was the
report to me later of several who were present), and
extreme kindness and hospitality from all the Wharton group. He rushed to Baltimore, and at midnight,
December 31, he wrote: "I had from eleven-thirty to
one P.M. an absolute supergrand talk with Adolph
Meyer and John Watson. He is a grand young south-
erner and simply knows his behavioristic psychology
in a way to make one's hair stand up. We talked my
plan clear out and they are *enthusiastic.* . . . Things
are going *grandly.*" Next day: "Just got in from dinner with Adolph Meyer. He is simply a wonder. . . .
At nine-thirty I watched Dr. Campbell give a girl
Freudian treatment for a suicide mania. She had been
a worker in a straw-hat factory and had a true industrial psychosis — the kind I am looking for." Then,
later: "There is absolutely no doubt that the trip
has been my making. I have learned a lot of back-
ground, things, and standards, that will put their
stamp on my development."

Almost every letter would tell of some one visit
which "alone was worth the trip East." Around
Christmastime home-longings got extra strong — he

wrote five letters in three days. I really wish I could quote some from them — where he said for instance: "My, but it is good for a fellow to be with his family and awful to be away from it." And again: "I want to be interrupted, I do. I'm all for that. I remember how Jim and Nand used to come into my study for a kiss and then go hastily out upon urgent affairs. I'm for that. . . . I've got my own folk and they make the rest of the world thin and pale. The blessedness of babies is beyond words, but the blessedness of a wife is such that one can't start in on it."

Then came the Economic Convention at Columbus — letters too full to begin to quote from them. "I'm simply having the time of my life . . . every one is here." In a talk when he was asked to fill in at the last minute, he presented "two arguments why trade-unions alone could not be depended on to bring desirable change in working conditions through collective bargaining: one, because they were numerically so few in contrast to the number of industrial workers, and, two, because the reforms about to be demanded were technical, medical, and generally of scientific character, and skilled experts employed by the state would be necessary."

Back again in New York, he wrote: "It just raises my hair to feel I'm not where a Dad ought to be. My blessed, precious family! I tell you there is n't anything in this world like a wife and babies and I'm for that life that puts me close. I'm near smart enough to last a heap of years. Though when I see how my trip makes me feel alive in my head and enthusiastic,

I know it has been worth while. . . ." Along in January he worked his thesis up in writing. "Last night I read my paper to the Robinsons after the dinner and they had Mr. and Mrs. John Dewey there. A most superb and grand discussion followed, the Deweys going home at eleven-thirty and I stayed to talk to one A.M. I slept dreaming wildly of the discussion. . . . Then had an hour and a half with Dewey on certain moot points. That talk was even more superb and resultful to me and I'm just about ready to quit. . . . I need now to write and read."

I quote a bit here and there from a paper written in New York in 1917, because, though hurriedly put together and never meant for publication, it describes Carl's newer approach to Economics and especially to the problem of Labor.

"In 1914 I was asked to investigate a riot among 2800 migratory hop-pickers in California which had resulted in five deaths, many-fold more wounded, hysteria, fear, and a strange orgy of irresponsible persecution by the county authorities — and, on the side of the laborers, conspiracy, barn-burnings, sabotage, and open revolutionary propaganda. I had been teaching labor-problems for a year, and had studied them in two American universities, under Sidney Webb in London, and in four universities of Germany. I found that I had no fundamentals which could be called good tools with which to begin my analysis of this riot. And I felt myself merely a conventional if astonished onlooker before the theoretically abnormal but manifestly natural emotional activity which swept over California. After what must have been a most usual intellectual cycle of, first, help-lessness, then conventional cataloguing, some ration-alizing, some moralizing, and an extensive feeling of shallowness and inferiority, I called the job done.

"By accident, somewhat later, I was loaned two books of Freud, and I felt after the reading, that I had found a scientific approach which might lead to the discovery of important fundamentals for a study of unrest and violence. Under this stimulation, I read, during a year and a half, general psychology, physi-ology and anthropology, eugenics, all the special material I could find on Mendelism, works on mental hygiene, feeblemindedness, insanity, evolution of morals and character, and finally found a resting-place in a field which seems to be best designated as Abnormal and Behavioristic Psychology. My quest throughout this experience seemed to be pretty stead-ily a search for those irreducible fundamentals which I could use in getting a technically decent opinion on that riot. In grand phrases, I was searching for the Scientific Standard of Value to be used in analyzing Human Behavior.

"Economics (which officially holds the analysis of labor-problems) has been allowed to devote itself almost entirely to the production of goods, and to neglect entirely the consumption of goods and human organic welfare. The lip-homage given by orthodox economics to the field of consumption seems to be inspired merely by the feeling that disaster might overcome production if workers were starved or business men discouraged. . . . So, while official economic science tinkers at its transient institutions which flourish in one decade and pass out in the next, abnormal and behavioristic psychology, physiology, psychiatry, are building in their laboratories, by induction from human specimens of modern economic life, a standard of human values and an elucidation of behavior fundamentals which alone we must use in our legislative or personal modification of modern civilization. It does not seem an overstatement to say that orthodox economics has cleanly overlooked two of the most important generalizations about human life which can be phrased, and those are, —

"That human life is dynamic, that change, movement, evolution, are its basic characteristics.

"That self-expression, and therefore freedom of choice and movement, are prerequisites to a satisfying human state."

After giving a description of the instincts he writes: —

"The importance to me of the following description of the innate tendencies or instincts lies in their relation to my main explanation of economic behavior which is, —

"First, that these tendencies are persistent, are far less warped or modified by the environment than we believe; that they function quite as they have for several hundred thousand years; that they, as motives, in their various normal or perverted habit-form, can at times dominate singly the entire behavior, and act as if they were a clear character dominant.

"Secondly, that if the environment through any of the conventional instruments of repression, such as religious orthodoxy, university mental discipline, economic inferiority, imprisonment, physical disfigurement, — such as short stature, hare-lip, etc., — repress the full psychological expression in the field of these tendencies, then a psychic revolt, slipping into abnormal mental functioning, takes place, and society accuses the revolutionist of being either willfully inefficient, alcoholic, a syndicalist, supersensitive, an agnostic, or insane."

I hesitate somewhat to give his programme as set forth in this paper. I have already mentioned that it was written in the spring of 1917, and hurriedly. In referring to this very paper in a letter from New York, he said, "Of course it is written in part *to call out* comments, and so the statements are strong and unmodified." Let that fact, then, be borne in mind, and also the fact that he may have altered his views somewhat in the light of his further studies and readings — although again, such studies may only have strengthened the following ideas. I cannot now trust to my memory for what discussions we may have had on the subject.

"Reform means a militant minority, or, to follow Trotter, a small Herd. This little Herd would give council, relief, and recuperation to its members. The members of the Herd will be under merciless fire from the convention-ridden members of general society. They will be branded outlaws, radicals, agnostics, impossible, crazy. They will be lucky to be out of jail most of the time. They will work by trial and study, gaining wisdom by their errors, as Sidney Webb and the Fabians did. In the end, after a long time, parts of the social sham will collapse, as it did in England, and small promises will become milestones of progress.

"From where, then, can we gain recruits for this minority? Two real sources seem in existence — the universities and the field of mental-disease speculation and hospital experiment. The one, the universities, with rare if wonderful exceptions, are fairly hopeless; the other is not only rich in promise, but few realize how full in performance. Most of the literature which is gripping that great intellectual no-man's land of the silent readers, is basing its appeal, and its story, on the rather uncolored and bald facts which come from Freud, Trotter, Robinson, Dewey, E. B. Holt, Lippmann, Morton Prince, Pierce, Bailey, Jung, Hart, Overstreet, Thorndike, Campbell, Meyer and Watson, Stanley Hall, Adler, White. It is from this field of comparative or abnormal psychology that the challenge to industrialism and the programme of change will come.

"But suppose you ask me to be concrete and give an idea of such a programme.

"Take simply the beginning of life, take childhood, for that is where the human material is least protected, most plastic, and where most injury to-day is done. In the way of general suggestion, I would say, exclude children from formal disciplinary life, such as that of all industry and most schools, up to the age of eighteen. After excluding them, what shall we do with them? Ask John Dewey, I suggest, or read his 'Schools of To-morrow,' or 'Democracy and Education.' It means tremendous, unprecedented money expense to ensure an active trial and error-learning activity; a chance naturally to recapitulate the racial trial and error-learning experience; a study and preparation of those periods of life in which fall the ripening of the relatively late maturing instincts; a general realizing that wisdom can come only from experience, and not from the Book. It means psychologically calculated childhood opportunity, in which the now stifled instincts of leadership, workmanship, hero-worship, hunting, migration, meditation, sex, could grow and take their foundation place in the psychic equipment of a biologically promising human being. To illustrate in trivialities, no father, with knowledge of the meaning of the universal bent towards workmanship, would give his son a puzzle if he knew of the Mecano or Erector toys, and no father would give the Mecano if he had grasped the educational potentiality of the gift to his child of $10 worth of lumber and a set of good carpenter's tools. There is now enough loose wisdom around devoted to childhood, its needed liberties and experiences, both to give the children of this civilization their first evolutionary chance, and to send most teachers back to the farm.

"In the age-period of 18 to 30 would fall that pseudo-educational monstrosity, the undergraduate university, and the degrading popular activities of 'beginning a business' or 'picking up a trade.' Much money must be spent here. Perhaps few fields of activity have been conventionalized as much as university education. Here, just where a superficial theorist would expect to find enthusiasm, emancipated minds, and hope, is found fear, convention, a mean instinct-life, no spirit of adventure, little curiosity, in general no promise of preparedness. No wonder philosophical idealism flourishes and Darwin is forgotten.

"The first two years of University life should be devoted to the Science of Human Behavior. Much of to-day's biology, zoölogy, history, if it is interpretive, psychology, if it is behavioristic, philosophy, if it is pragmatic, literature, if it had been written involuntarily, would find its place here. The last two years could be profitably spent in appraising with that ultimate standard of value gained in the first two years, the various institutions and instruments used by civilized man. All instruction would be objective, scientific, and emancipated from convention — wonderful prospect!

"In industrial labor and in business employments a new concept, a new going philosophy must be unreservedly accepted, which has, instead of the ideal of forcing the human beings to mould their habits to assist the continued existence of the inherited order of things, an ideal of moulding all business institutions and ideas of prosperity in the interests of scientific evolutionary aims and large human pleasures. As Pigou has said, 'Environment has its children as well as men.' Monotony in labor, tedium in office-work, time spent in business correspondence, the boredom of running a sugar refinery, would be asked to

step before the bar of human affairs and get a health
standardization. To-day industry produces goods
that cost more than they are worth, are consumed
by persons who are degraded by the consuming; it
is destroying permanently the raw-material source
which, science has painfully explained, could be made
inexhaustible. Some intellectual revolution must come
which will *de*-emphasize business and industry and
re-emphasize most other ways of self-expression.

"In Florence, around 1300, Giotto painted a picture, and the day it was to be hung in St. Mark's, the
town closed down for a holiday, and the people, with
garlands of flowers and songs, escorted the picture
from the artist's studio to the church. Three weeks
ago I stood, in company with 500 silent, sallow-faced
men, at a corner on Wall Street, a cold and wet corner,
till young Morgan issued from J. P. Morgan & Company, and walked 20 feet to his carriage. — We produce, probably, per capita, 1000 times more in weight
of ready-made clothing, Irish lace, artificial flowers,
terra cotta, movie-films, telephones, and printed matter than those Florentines did, but we have, with our
100,000,000 inhabitants, yet to produce that little
town, her Dante, her Andrea del Sarto, her Michael
Angelo, her Leonardo da Vinci, her Savonarola, her
Giotto, or the group who followed Giotto's picture.
Florence had a marvelous energy — re-lease experience. All our industrial formalism, our conventionalized young manhood, our schematized universities,
are instruments of balk and thwart, are machines to
produce protesting abnormality, to block efficiency.

So the problem of industrial labor is one with the problem of the discontented business man, the indifferent student, the unhappy wife, the immoral minister — it is one of maladjustment between a fixed human nature and a carelessly ordered world. The result is suffering, insanity, racial-perversion, and danger. The final cure is gaining acceptance for a new standard of morality; the first step towards this is to break down the mores-inhibitions to free experimental thinking."

If only the time had been longer — if only the Book itself could have been finished! For he *had* a great message. He was writing about a thousand words a day on it the following summer, at Castle Crags, when the War Department called him into mediation work and not another word did he ever find time to add to it. It stands now about one third done. I shall get that third ready for publication, together with some of his shorter articles. There have been many who have offered their services in completing the Book, but the field is so new, Carl's contribution so unique, that few men in the whole country understand the ground enough to be of service. It was not so much to be a book on Labor as on Labor-Psychology — and that is almost an unexplored field.

CHAPTER XII

THREE days after Carl started east, on his arrival in Seattle, President Suzzallo called him to the University of Washington as Head of the Department of Economics and Dean of the College of Business Administration, his work to begin the following autumn. It seemed an ideal opportunity. He wrote: "I am very, very attracted by Suzzallo. . . . He said that I should be allowed to plan the work as I wished and call the men I wished, and could call at least five. I cannot imagine a better man to work with nor a better proposition than the one he put up to me. . . . The job itself will let me teach what I wish and in my own way. I can give Introductory Economics, and Labor, and Industrial Organization, etc." Later, he telegraphed from New York, where he had again seen Suzzallo: "Have accepted Washington's offer. . . . Details of job even more satisfactory than before."

So, sandwiched in between all the visits and interviews over the Book, were many excursions about locating new men for the University of Washington. I like to think of what the three Pennsylvania men he wanted had to say about him. Seattle seemed very far away to them — they were doubtful, very. Then they heard the talk before the Conference referred to above, and every one of the three accepted his call. As one of them expressed it to his wife later: "I'd go anywhere for that man." Between that Seattle call and his death there were eight universities, some of them the biggest in the country, which wished Carl Parker to be on their faculties. One smaller university held out the presidency to him. Besides this, there were nine jobs outside of University work that were offered him, from managing a large mine to doing research work in Europe. He had come into his own.

It was just before we left Berkeley that the University of California asked Carl to deliver an address, explaining his approach to economics. It was, no doubt, the most difficult talk he ever gave. There under his very nose sat his former colleagues, his fellow members in the Economics Department, and he had to stand up in public and tell them just how inadequate he felt most of their teaching to be. The head of the Department came in a trifle late and left immediately after the lecture. He could hardly have been expected to include himself in the group who gathered later around Carl to express their interest in his stand. I shall quote a bit from this paper to show Carl's ideas on orthodox economics.

"This brings one to perhaps the most costly delinquency of modern Economics, and that is its refusal to incorporate into its weighings and appraisals the facts and hypotheses of modern psychology. Nothing in the postulates of the science of Economics is as ludicrous as its catalogue of human wants. Though the practice of ascribing 'faculties' to man has been passed by psychology into deserved discard, Economics still maintains, as basic human qualities, a galaxy of vague and rather spiritual faculties. It matters not

that, in the place of the primitive concepts of man
stimulated to activity by a single trucking sense, or a
free and uninfluenced force called a soul, or a 'desire
for financial independence,' psychology has established a human being possessed of more instincts than
any animal, and with a psychical nature whose activities fall completely within the causal law.

"It would be a great task and a useless one to work
through current economic literature and gather the
strange and mystical collection of human dispositions
which economists have named the springs of human
activity. They have no relation to the modern re-
searches into human behavior of psychology or physi-
ology. They have an interesting relation only to the
moral attributes postulated in current religion.

"But more important and injurious than the cari-
caturing of wants has been the disappearance from
Economics of any treatment or interest in human
behavior and the evolution of human character in
Economic life. This is explained in large part by the
self-divorce of Economics from the biological field;
but also in an important way by the exclusion from
Economics of considerations of consumption.

"Only under the influence of the social and educational psychologists and behaviorists could child-
labor, the hobo, unemployment, poverty, and criminality be given their just emphasis; and it seems
accurate to ascribe the social sterility of Economic
theory and its programme to its ignorance and lack
of interest in modern comparative psychology.

"A deeper knowledge of human instincts would

never have allowed American economists to keep
their faith in a simple rise of wages as an all-cure for
labor unrest. In England, with a homogeneous labor
class, active in politics, maintaining university extension courses, spending their union's income on intri-
cate betterment schemes, and wealthy in tradition —
there a rise in wages meant an increase in welfare.
But in the United States, with a heterogeneous labor
class, bereft of their social norms by the violence of
their uprooting from the old world, dropped into an
unprepared and chaotic American life, with its insidi-
ous prestige — here a rise in wages could and does
often mean added ostentation, social climbing, superficial polishing, new vice. This social perversion
in the consuming of the wage-increase is without the
ken of the economist. He cannot, if he would, think
of it, for he has no mental tools, no norms applicable
for entrance into the medley of human motives called
consumption.

"For these many reasons economic thinking has
been weak and futile in the problems of conservation,
of haphazard invention, of unrestricted advertising,
of anti-social production, of the inadequacy of income,
of criminality. These are problems within the zone of
the intimate life of the population. They are economic
problems, and determine efficiencies within the whole
economic life. The divorcing for inspection of the field
of production from the rest of the machinery of civilization has brought into practice a false method, and
the values arrived at have been unhappily half-truths.
America to-day is a monument to the truth that

growth in wealth becomes significant for national welfare only when it is joined with an efficient and social
policy in its consumption.

"Economics will only save itself through an alliance
with the sciences of human behavior, psychology, and
biology, and through a complete emancipation from
'prosperity mores.' . . . The sin of Economics has been
the divorce of its work from reality, of announcing an
analysis of human activity with the human element
left out."

One other point remained ever a sore spot with
Carl, and that was the American university and its
accomplishments. In going over his writings, I find
scattered through the manuscripts explosions on the
ways, means, and ends, of academic education in our
United States. For instance, —

"Consider the paradox of the rigidity of the university student's scheme of study, and the vagaries
and whims of the scholarly emotion. Contemplate
the forcing of that most delicate of human attributes,
i.e., interest, to bounce forth at the clang of a gong.
To illustrate: the student is confidently expected to
lose himself in fine contemplation of Plato's philosophy up to eleven o'clock, and then at 11.07, with
no important mental cost, to take up a profitable and
scholarly investigation into the banking problems of
the United States. He will be allowed by the proper
academic committee German Composition at one
o'clock, diseases of citrus fruit trees at two, and at
three he is asked to exhibit a fine sympathy in the
Religions and Customs of the Orient. Between 4.07

and five it is calculated that he can with profit indulge in gymnasium recreation, led by an instructor who counts out loud and waves his arms in time to a mechanical piano. Between five and six, this student, led by a yell-leader, applauds football practice. The growing tendency of American university students to spend their evenings in extravagant relaxation, at the moving pictures, or in unconventional dancing, is said to be willful and an indication of an important moral sag of recent years. It would be interesting also to know if Arkwright, Hargreaves, Watt, or Darwin, Edison, Henry Ford, or the Wrights, or other persons of desirable if unconventional mechanical imagination, were encouraged in their scientific meditation by scholastic experiences of this kind. Every American university has a department of education devoted to establishing the most effective methods of imparting knowledge to human beings."

From the same article: —

"The break in the systematization which an irregular and unpredictable thinker brings arouses a persistent if unfocused displeasure. Hence we have the accepted and cultivated institutions, such as our universities, our churches, our clubs, sustaining with care mediocre standards of experimental thought. European critics have long compared the repressed and uninspiring intellect of the American undergraduate with the mobile state of mind of the Russian and German undergraduates which has made their institutions the centre of revolutionary change propaganda. To one who knows in any intimate way the life of the American student, it becomes only an uncomfortable humor to visualize any of his campuses as the origins of social protests. The large industry of American college athletics and its organization-for-victory concept, the tendency to set up an efficient corporation as the proper university model, the extensive and unashamed university advertising, and consequent apprehension of public opinion, the love of size and large registration, that strange psychological abnormality, organized cheering, the curious companionship of state universities and military drill, regular examinations and rigidly prescribed work — all these interesting characteristics are, as is natural in character-formation, both cause and effect. It becomes an easy prophecy within behaviorism to forecast that American universities will continue regular and mediocre in mental activity and reasonably devoid of intellectual bent toward experimental thinking."

Perhaps here is where I may quote a letter Carl received just before leaving Berkeley, and his answer to it. This correspondence brings up several points on which Carl at times received criticism, and I should like to give the two sides, each so typical of the point of view it represents.

February 28, 1917

MY DEAR CARLETON PARKER, —

When we so casually meet it is as distressing as it is amusing to me, to know that the God I intuitively defend presents to you the image of the curled and scented monster of the Assyrian sculpture.

He was never that to me, and the visualization of an imaginative child is a remarkable thing. From the first, the word "God," spoken in the comfortable (almost smug) atmosphere of the old Unitarian congregation, took my breath and tranced me into a vision of a great flood of vibrating light, and *only* light.

I wonder if, in your childhood, some frightening picture in some old book was not the thing that you are still fighting against? So that, emancipated as you are, you are still a little afraid, and must perforce — with a remainder of the brave swagger of youth — set up a barrier of authorities to fight behind, and, quite unconsciously, you are thus building yourself into a vault in which no flowers can bloom — because you have sealed the high window of the imagination so that the frightening God may not look in upon you — this same window through which simple men get an illumination that saves their lives, and in the light of which they communicate kindly, one with the other, their faith and hopes?

I am impelled to say this to you, first, because of the responsibility which rests upon you in your relation to young minds; and, second, I like you and your eagerness and the zest for Truth that you transmit.

You are dedicated to the pursuit of Truth, and you afford us the dramatic incidents of your pursuit.

Yet up to this moment it seems to me you are accepting Truth at second-hand.

I counted seventeen "authorities" quoted, chapter and verse (and then abandoned the enumeration), in the free talk of the other evening; and asked myself if this reverence of the student for the master, was all that we were ultimately to have of that vivid individual whom we had so counted upon as Carl Parker?

I wondered, too, if, in the great opportunity that has come to you, those simple country boys and girls of Washington were to be thus deprived, — were to find not you but your "authorities," — because Carl Parker refused (even ever so modestly) to learn that Truth, denied the aid of the free imagination, takes revenge upon her disciple, by shutting off from him the sources of life by which a man is made free, and reducing his mind — his rich, variable, potential mind — to the mechanical operation of a repetitious machine.

I feel this danger for you, and for the youths you are to educate, so poignantly that I venture to write with this frankness.

Your present imprisonment is not necessarily a life sentence; but your satisfaction in it — your acceptance of the routine of your treadmill — is chilling to the hopes of those who have waited upon your progress; and it imperils your future — as well as that hope we have in the humanities that are to be implanted in the minds of the young people you are to instruct. We would not have you remain under the misapprehension that Truth alone can ever serve humanity — Truth remains sterile until it is married to Goodness. That marriage is consummated in the high flight of the imagination, and its progeny is of beauty.

You need beauty — you need verse and color and

music — you need all the escapes — all the doors
wide open — and this seemingly impertinent letter
is merely the appeal of one human creature to another, for the sake of all the human creatures whom
you have it in your power to endow with chains or
with wings.

Very sincerely yours,
BRUCE PORTER.

MY DEAR BRUCE PORTER, —

My present impatient attitude towards a mystic
being without doubt has been influenced by some
impression of my childhood, but not the terror-
bringing creatures you suggest. My family was one
of the last three which clung to a dying church in my
country town. I, though a boy of twelve, passed the
plate for two years while the minister's daughter sang
a solo. Our village was not a happy one, and the in-
congruity of our emotional prayers and ecstasies of
imagery, and the drifting dullness and meanness of
the life outside, filtered in some way into my boy
mind. I saw that suffering was real and pressing, and
so many suffered resignedly; and that imagery and my
companionship with a God (I was highly "religious"
then) worked in a self-centred circle. I never strayed
from the deadly taint of some gentle form of egotism.
I was then truly in a "vault." I did things for a system
of ethics, not because of a fine rush of social brotherly
intuition. My imagination was ever concerned with
me and my prospects, my salvation. I honestly and
soberly believe that your "high window of the imag-

ination" works out in our world as such a force for
egotism; it is a self-captivating thing, it divorces man
from the plain and bitter realities of life, it brings an
anti-social emancipation to him. I can sincerely make
this terrible charge against the modern world, and
that is, that it is its bent towards mysticism, its
blinding itself through hysteria, which makes possible
in its civilization its desperate inequalities of life-
expression, its tortured children, its unhappy men
and women, its wasted potentiality. We have not
been humble and asked what is man; we have not
allowed ourselves to weigh sorrow. It is in such a use
that our powers of imagination could be brotherly.
We look on high in ecstasy, and fail to be on flame
because of the suffering of those whose wounds are
bare to our eyes on the street.

And that brings me to my concept of a God. God
exists in us because of our bundle of social brother-
acts. Contemplation and crying out and assertions of
belief are in the main notices that we are substituting
something for acts. Our God should be a thing discovered only in retrospect. We live, we fight, we know
others, and, as Overstreet says, our God sins and
fights at our shoulder. He may be a mean God or a
fine one. He is limited in his stature by our service.

I fear your God, because I think he is a product of
the unreal and unhelpful, that he has a " bad psychological past," that he is subtly egotistical, that he fills
the vision and leaves no room for the simple and
patient deeds of brotherhood, a heavenly contemplation taking the place of earthly deeds.

You feel that I quote too many minds and am hobbled by it. I delight just now in the companionship of men through their books. I am devoted to knowing the facts of the lives of other humans and the train of thought which their experiences have started. To lead them is like talking to them. I suspect, even dread, the "original thinker" who knows little of the experiments and failures of the thinkers of other places and times. To me such a stand denies that promising thing, the evolution of human thought. I also turn from those who borrow, but neglect to tell their sources. I want my "simple boys and girls of Washington" to know that to-day is a day of honest science; that events have antecedents; that "luck" does not exist; that the world will improve only through thoughtful social effort, and that lives are happy only in that effort. And with it all there will be time for beauty and verse and color and music — far be it from me to shut these out of my own life or the lives of others. But they are instruments, not attributes. I am very glad you wrote.

Sincerely yours,

CARLETON H. PARKER.

CHAPTER XIII

In May we sold our loved hill nest in Berkeley and started north, stopping for a three months' vacation — our first real vacation since we had been married — at Castle Crags, where, almost ten years before, we had spent the first five days of our honeymoon, before going into Southern Oregon. There, in a log-cabin among the pines, we passed unbelievably cherished days — work a-plenty, play a-plenty, and the family together day in, day out. There was one little extra trip he got in with the two sons, for which I am so thankful. The three of them went off with their sleeping-bags and rods for two days, leaving "the girls" behind. Each son caught his first trout with a fly. They put the fish, cleaned, in a cool sheltered spot, because they had to be carried home for me to see; and lo! a little bear came down in the night and ate the fish, in addition to licking the fat all off the frying-pan.

Then, like a bolt from the blue, came the fateful telegram from Washington, D.C. — labor difficulties in construction-work at Camp Lewis — would he report there at once as Government Mediator. Oh! the Book, the Book — the Book that was to be finished without fail before the new work at the University of Washington began! Perhaps he would be back in a week! Surely he would be back in a week! So he packed just enough for a week, and off he went.

One week! When, after four weeks, there was still no let up in his mediation duties, — in fact they increased, — I packed up the family and we left for Seattle. I had rewound his fishing-rod with orange silk, and had revarnished it, as a surprise for his home-coming to Castle Crags. He never fished with it again.

How that man loved fishing! How he loved every sport, for that matter. And he loved them with the same thoroughness and allegiance that he gave to any cause near his heart. Baseball — he played on his high-school team (also he could recite "Casey at the Bat" with a gusto that many a friend of the earlier days will remember. And here I am reminded of his "Christopher Columnibus." I recently ran across a postcard a college mate sent Carl from Italy years ago, with a picture of a statue of Columbus on it. On the reverse side the friend had written, quoting from Carl's monologue: "'Boom Joe!' says the king; which is being interpreted, 'I see you first.' 'Wheat cakes,' says Chris, which is the Egyptian for 'Boom Joe'"). He loved football, track, — he won three gold medals broad-jumping, — canoeing, swimming, billiards, — he won a loving cup at that, — tennis, ice-skating, hand-ball; and yes, ye of finer calibre, quiver if you will — he loved a prize-fight and played a mighty good game of poker, as well as bridge — though in the ten and a half years that we were married I cannot remember that he played poker once or bridge more than five times. He did, however, enjoy his bridge with Simon Patton in Philadelphia; and when he played, he played well.

I tell you there was hardly anything the man could not do. He could draw the funniest pictures you ever saw — I wish I could reproduce the letters he sent his sons from the East. He was a good carpenter — the joy it meant to his soul to add a second-hand tool ever so often to his collection! Sunday morning was special carpenter-time — new shelves here, a bookcase there, new steps up to the swimming-tank, etc. I have heard many a man say that he told a story better than any one they ever heard. He was an expert woodsman. And, my gracious! how he did love babies! That hardly fits in just here, but I think of it now. His love for children colored his whole economic viewpoint.

"There is the thing that possessed Parker — the perception of the destructive significance of the repressed and balked instincts of the migratory worker, the unskilled, the casuals, the hoboes, the womanless, jobless, voteless men. To him their tragedy was akin to the tragedy of child-life in our commercialized cities. More often than of anything else, he used to talk to me of the fatuous blindness of a civilization that centred its economic activities in places where child-life was perpetually repressed and imperiled. The last time I saw him he was flaming indignation at the ghastly record of children killed and maimed by trucks and automobiles. What business had automobiles where children should be free to play? What could be said for the human wisdom of a civilization that placed traffic above child-life? In our denial to children, to millions of men and women, of the means for satisfying their instinctive desires and innate dispositions, he saw the principal explanation of crime, labor-unrest, the violence of strikes, the ghastly violence of war."[1]

He could never pass any youngster anywhere without a word of greeting as from friend to friend. I remember being in a crowded car with him in our engaged days. He was sitting next to a woman with a baby who was most unhappy over the ways of the world. Carl asked if he could not hold the squaller. The mother looked a bit doubtful, but relinquished her child. Within two minutes the babe was content on Carl's knees, clutching one of his fingers in a fat fist and sucking his watch. The woman leaned over to me later, as she was about to depart with a very sound asleep offspring. "Is he as lovely as that to his own?"

The tenderness of him over his own! Any hour of the day or night he was alert to be of any service in any trouble, big or little. He had a collection of tricks and stories on hand for any youngster who happened along. The special pet of our own boys was "The Submarine Obo Bird" — a large flapper (Dad's arms fairly rent the air), which was especially active early in the morning, when small boys appeared to prefer staying in bed to getting up. The Obo Bird went "Pak! Pak!" and lit on numerous objects about the sleeping porch. Carl's two hands would plump stiff, fingers down, on the railing, or on a small screw sticking out somewhere. Scratches. Then "Pak!" and more flaps. This time the Obo Bird would light a trifle

[1] Robert Bruère, in the *New Republic*, May 18, 1918.

nearer the small boy whose "turn" it was — round eyes, and an agitated grin from ear to ear, plus explosive giggles and gurglings emerging from the covers. Nearer and nearer came the Obo Bird. Gigglier and gigglier got the small boy. Finally, with a spring and a last "Pak! Pak! Pak!" the Obo Bird dove under the covers at the side of the bed and pinched the small boy who would not get up. (Rather a premium on not rising promptly was the Obo Bird.) Final ecstatic squeals from the pinched. Then, "Now it's my turn, daddo!" from the other son. — The Submarine Obo Bird lived in Alaska and ate Spooka biscuits. There was just developing a wee Obo Bird, that made less vehement "paks!" and pinched less agitatedly — a special June-Bug Obo Bird. In fact, the baby was not more than three months old when the boys demanded a Submarine Obo Bird that ate little Spooka biscuits for sister.

His trip to Camp Lewis threw him at once into the midst of the lumber difficulties of the Northwest, which lasted for months. The big strike in the lumber industry was on when he arrived. He wrote: "It is a strike to better conditions. The I.W.W. are only the display feature. The main body of opinion is from a lot of unskilled workers who are sick of the filthy bunk-houses and rotten grub." He wrote later of a conference with the big lumbermen, and of how they would not stay on the point but "roared over the I.W.W. I told them that condemnation was not a solution, or businesslike, but what we wanted was a statement of how they were to open their plants. More roars. More demands for troops, etc. I said I was a college man, not used to business; but if business men had as much trouble as this keeping to the real points involved, give me a faculty analysis. They laughed over this and got down to business, and in an hour lined up the affair in mighty good shape."

I wish it were proper to go into the details here of the various conferences, the telegrams sent to Washington, the replies. Carl wrote: "I am saving all the copies for you, as it is most interesting history." Each letter would end: "By three days at least I should start back. I am getting frantic to be home." Home, for the Parkers, was always where we happened to be then. Castle Crags was as much "home" as any place had ever been. We had moved fourteen times in ten years: of the eleven Christmases we had had together, only two had been in the same place. There were times when "home" was a Pullman car. It made no difference. One of the strange new feelings I have to get used to is the way I now look at places to live in. It used to be that Carl and I, in passing the littlest bit of a hovel, would say, "We could be perfectly happy in a place like that, could n't we? Nothing makes any difference if we are together." But certain kinds of what we called "cuddly" houses used to make us catch our breaths, to think of the extra joy it would be living together tucked away in there. Now, when I pass a place that looks like that, I have to drop down some kind of a trap-door in my brain, and not think at all until I get well by it.

Labor conditions in the Northwest grew worse, strikes more general, and finally Carl wrote that he just must be indefinitely on the job. "I am so homesick for you that I feel like packing up and coming. I literally feel terribly. But with all this feeling I don't see how I can. Not only have I been telegraphed to stay on the job, but the situation is growing steadily worse. Last night my proposal (eight-hour day, nonpartisan complaint and adjustment board, suppression of violence by the state) was turned down by the operators in Tacoma. President Suzzallo and I fought for six hours but it went down. The whole situation is drifting into a state of incipient sympathetic strikes." Later: "This is the most bull-headed affair and I don't think it is going to get anywhere." Still later: "Things are not going wonderfully in our mediation. Employers demanding everything and men granting much but not that." Again: "Each day brings a new crisis. Gee, labor is unrestful . . . and gee, the pigheadedness of bosses! Human nature is sure one hundred per cent psychology." Also he wrote, referring to the general situation at the University and in the community: "Am getting absolutely crazy with enthusiasm over my job here. . . . It is too vigorous and resultful for words." And again: "The mediation between employers and men blew up to-day at 4 P.M. and now a host of nice new strikes show on the horizon. . . . There are a lot of fine operators but some hard shells." Again: "Gee, I'm learning! And talk about material for the Book!"

An article appeared in one of the New York papers

recently, entitled "How Carleton H. Parker Settled Strikes": —

"It was under his leadership that, in less than a year, twenty-seven disputes which concerned Government work in the Pacific Northwest were settled, and it was his method to lay the basis for permanent relief as he went along. . . .

"Parker's contribution was in the method he used. . . . Labor leaders of all sorts would flock to him in a bitter, weltering mass, mouthing the set phrases of class-hatred they use so effectually in stirring up trouble. They would state their case. And Parker would quietly deduce the irritation points that seemed to stand out in the jumbled testimony.

"Then it would be almost laughable to the observer to hear the employer's side of the case. Invariably it was just as bitter, just as unreasoning, and just as violent, as the statement of their case by the workers. Parker would endeavor to find, in all this heap of words, the irritation points of the other side.

"But when a study was finished, his diagnosis made, and his prescription of treatment completed, Parker always insisted in carrying it straight to the workers. And he did not just tell them results. He often took several hours, sometimes several meetings of several hours each. In these meetings he would go over every detail of his method, from start to finish, explaining, answering questions, meeting objections with reason. And he always won them over. But, of course, it must be said that he had a tremendously compelling personality that carried him far."

CHAPTER XIV

At the end of August the little family was united again in Seattle. Almost the clearest picture of Carl I have is the eager look with which he scanned the people stepping out of our car at the station, and the beam that lit up his face as he spied us. There is a line in Dorothy Canfield's "Bent Twig" that always appealed to us. The mother and father were separated for a few days, to the utter anguish of the father especially, and he remarked, "It's Hell to be happily married!" Every time we were ever separated we felt just that.

In one of Carl's letters from Seattle he had written: "The 'Atlantic Monthly' wants me to write an article on the I.W.W.!!" So the first piece of work he had to do after we got settled was that. We were tremendously excited, and never got over chuckling at some of the moss-grown people we knew about the country who would feel outraged at the "Atlantic Monthly" stooping to print stuff by that young radical. And on such a subject! How we tore at the end, to get the article off on time! The stenographer from the University came about two one Sunday afternoon. I sat on the floor up in the guest-room and read the manuscript to her while she typed it off. Carl would rush down more copy from his study on the third floor. I'd go over it while Miss Van Doren went over what she had typed. Then the reading would begin again.

We hated to stop for supper, all three of us were so excited to get the job done. It *had* to be at the main post-office that night by eleven, to arrive in Boston when promised. At ten-thirty it was in the envelope, three limp people tore for the car, we put Miss Van Doren on, — she was to mail the article on her way home, — and Carl and I, knowing this was an occasion for a treat if ever there was one, routed out a sleepy drug-store clerk and ate the remains of his Sunday ice-cream supply.

I can never express how grateful I am that that article was written and published before Carl died. The influence of it ramified in many and the most unexpected directions. I am still hearing of it. We expected condemnation at the time. There probably was plenty of it, but only one condemner wrote. On the other hand, letters streamed in by the score from friends and strangers bearing the general message, "God bless you for it!"

That article is particularly significant as showing his method of approach to the whole problem of the I.W.W., after some two years of psychological study.

"The futility of much conventional American social analysis is due to its description of the given problem in terms of its relationship to some relatively unimportant or artificial institution. Few of the current analyses of strikes or labor violence make use of the basic standards of human desire and intention which control these phenomena. A strike and its demands are usually praised as being law-abiding, or economically bearable, or are condemned as being unlawful, or confiscatory. These four attributes of a strike are important only as incidental consequences. The habit of Americans thus to measure up social problems to the current, temporary, and more or less accidental scheme of traditions and legal institutions, long ago gave birth to our national belief that passing a new law or forcing obedience to an old one was a specific for any unrest. The current analysis of the I.W.W. and its activities is an example of this perverted and unscientific method. The I.W.W. analysis, which has given both satisfaction and a basis for treating the organization, runs as follows: the organization is un-lawful in its activity, un-American in its sabotage, unpatriotic in its relation to the flag, the government, and the war. The rest of the condemnation is a play upon these three attributes. So proper and so suffi-cient has this condemnatory analysis become, that it is a risky matter to approach the problem from an-other angle. But it is now so obvious that our internal affairs are out of gear, that any comprehensive scheme of national preparedness would demand that full and honest consideration be given to all forces determin-ing the degree of American unity, one force being this tabooed organization.

"It would be best to announce here a more or less dogmatic hypothesis to which the writer will stead-fastly adhere: that human behavior results from the rather simple, arithmetical combination of the in-herited nature of man and the environment in which his maturing years are passed. Man will behave according to the hints for conduct which the accidents of his life have stamped into his memory mechanism. A slum produces a mind which has only slum incidents with which to work, and a spoiled and protected child seldom rises to aggressive competitive behavior, simply because its past life has stored up no memory imprints from which a predisposition to vigorous life can be built. The particular things called the moral attributes of man's conduct are conventionally found by contrasting this educated and trained way of acting with the exigencies and social needs or dangers of the time. Hence, while his immoral or unpatriotic behavior may fully justify his government in imprisoning or eliminating him when it stands in some particular danger which his conduct intensifies, this punishment in no way either explains his character or points to an enduring solution of his problem. Suppression, while very often justified and necessary in the flux of human relationship, always carries a social cost which must be liquidated, and also a backfire danger which must be insured against. The human being is born with no innate proclivity to crime or special kind of unpatriotism. Crime and treason are habit-activities, educated into man by environmental influences favorable to their development. . . .

"The I.W.W. can be profitably viewed only as a psychological by-product of the neglected childhood of industrial America. It is discouraging to see the problem to-day examined almost exclusively from the point of view of its relation to patriotism and conventional commercial morality. . . .

"It is perhaps of value to quote the language of the most influential of the I.W.W. leaders.

"'You ask me why the I.W.W. is not patriotic to the United States. If you were a bum without a blanket; if you left your wife and kids when you went West for a job, and had never located them since; if your job never kept you long enough in a place to qualify you to vote; if you slept in a lousy, sour bunk-house, and ate food just as rotten as they could give you and get by with it; if deputy sheriffs shot your cooking-cans full of holes and spilled your grub on the ground; if your wages were lowered on you when the bosses thought they had you down; if there was one law for Ford, Suhr, and Mooney, and another for Harry Thaw; if every person who represented law and order and the nation beat you up, railroaded you to jail, and the good Christian people cheered and told them to go to it, how in hell do you expect a man to be patriotic? This war is a business man's war and we don't see why we should go out and get shot in order to save the lovely state of affairs that we now enjoy.'

"The argument was rather difficult to keep productive, because gratitude — that material prerequisite to patriotism — seemed wanting in their attitude toward the American government. Their state of mind could be explained only by referring it, as was earlier suggested, to its major relationships. The dominating concern of the I.W.W. is what Keller calls the maintenance problem. Their philosophy is, in its simple reduction, a stomach-philosophy, and their politico-industrial revolt could be called without injustice a hunger-riot. But there is an important correction to this simple statement. While their way of living has seriously encroached on the urgent minima of nutrition, shelter, clothing, and physical health, it has also long outraged the American laboring-class traditions touching social life, sex-life, self-dignity, and ostentation. Had the food and shelter been sufficient, the revolt tendencies might have simmered out, were the migratory labor population not keenly sensitive to traditions of a richer psychological life than mere physical maintenance."

The temper of the country on this subject, the general closed attitude of mind which the average man holds thereon, prompt me to add here a few more of Carl's generalizations and conclusions in this article. If only he were here, to cry aloud again and yet again on this point! Yet I know there are those who sense his approach, and are endeavoring in every way possible to make wisdom prevail over prejudice.

"Cynical disloyalty and contempt of the flag must, in the light of modern psychology, come from a mind which is devoid of national gratitude, and in which the United States stirs no memory of satisfaction or happiness. To those of us who normally feel loyal to the nation, such a disloyal sentiment brings sharp indignation. As an index of our own sentiment and our own happy relations to the nation, this indignation has value. As a stimulus to a programme or ethical generalization, it is the cause of vast inaccuracy and sad injustice. American syndicalism is not a scheming group dominated by an unconventional and destructive social philosophy. It is merely a commonplace attitude — not such a state of mind as Machiavelli or Robespierre possessed, but one stamped by the lowest, most miserable labor-conditions and outlook which American industrialism produces. To those who have seen at first-hand the life of the western casual laborer, any reflections on his gratitude or spiritual buoyancy seem ironical humor.

"An altogether unwarranted importance has been given to the syndicalist philosophy of the I.W.W. A few leaders use its phraseology. Of these few, not half a dozen know the meaning of French syndicalism or English guild socialism. To the great wandering rank and file, the I.W.W. is simply the only social break in the harsh search for work that they have ever had; its headquarters the only competitor of the saloon in which they are welcome. . . .

"It is a conventional economic truism that American industrialism is guaranteeing to some half of the forty millions of our industrial population a life of such limited happiness, of such restrictions on personal development, and of such misery and desolation when sickness or accident comes, that we should be childish political scientists not to see that from such an environment little self-sacrificing love of country, little of ethics, little of gratitude could come. It is unfortunate that the scientific findings of our social condition must use words which sound strangely like the phraseology of the Socialists. This similarity, however, should logically be embarrassing to the critics of these findings, not to the scientists. Those who have investigated and studied the lower strata of American labor have long recognized the I.W.W. as purely a symptom of a certain distressing state of affairs. The casual migratory laborers are the finished product of an economic environment which seems cruelly efficient in turning out human beings modeled after all the standards which society abhors. The history of the migratory workers shows that, starting with the long hours and dreary winters on the farms they ran away from, or the sour-smelling bunk-house in a coal village, through their character-debasing experience with the drifting 'hire and fire' life in the industries, on to the vicious social and economic life of the winter unemployed, their training predetermined but one outcome, and the environment produced its type.

"The I.W.W. has importance only as an illustration of a stable American economic process. Its pitiful syndicalism, its street-corner opposition to the war, are the inconsequential trimmings. Its strike alone, faithful as it is to the American type, is an illuminating thing. The I.W.W., like the Grangers, the Knights of Labor, the Farmers' Alliance, the Progressive Party, is but a phenomenon of revolt. The cure lies in taking care of its psychic antecedents; the stability of our Republic depends on the degree of courage and wisdom with which we move to the task."

In this same connection I quote from another article: —

"No one doubts the full propriety of the govern-

ment's suppressing ruthlessly any interference of the
I.W.W. with war-preparation. All patriots should
just as vehemently protest against all suppression of
the normal protest activities of the I.W.W. There
will be neither permanent peace nor prosperity in our
country till the revolt basis of the I.W.W. is removed.
And until that is done, the I.W.W. remains an unfortunate, valuable symptom of a diseased industrialism."

I watch, along with many others, the growth of
bitterness and hysteria in the treatment of labor
spreading throughout our country, and I long, with
many others, for Carl, with his depth and sanity of
understanding, coupled with his passion for justice
and democracy, to be somewhere in a position of
guidance for these troublous times.

I am reminded here of a little incident that took
place just at this time. An I.W.W. was to come out
to have dinner with us — some other friends, faculty
people, also were to be there. About noon the telephone rang. Carl went. A rich Irish brogue announced:
"R—— can't come to your party to-night." "Why is
that?" "He's pinched. An' he wants t' know can he
have your Kant's 'Critique of Pure Reason' to read
while he's in jail."

CHAPTER XV

I AM forever grateful that Carl had his experience at
the University of Washington before he died. He left
the University of California a young Assistant Professor, just one rebellious morsel in a huge machine.
He found himself in Washington, not only Head of
the Department of Economics and Dean of the College of Commerce, and a power on the campus, but a
power in the community as well. He was working
under a President who backed him in everything to
the last ditch, who was keenly interested in every
ambition he had for making a big thing of his work.
He at last could see Introductory Economics given as
he wanted to have it given — realizing at the same
time that his plans were in the nature of an experiment. The two textbooks used in the first semester
were McDougall's "Social Psychology" and Wallas's
"Great Society." During part of the time he pinned
the front page of the morning paper on the board,
and illustrated his subject-matter by an item of news
of that very day.

His theory of education was that the first step in
any subject was to awaken a keen interest and curiosity in the student; for that reason he felt that pure
theory in Economics was too difficult for any but
seniors or graduates; that, given too soon, it tended
only to discourage. He allowed no note-taking in any
of his courses, insisted on discussion by the class, no

matter how large it was, planned to do away with written examinations as a test of scholarship, substituting instead a short oral discussion with each student individually, grading them "passed" and "not passed." As it was, because of the pressure of Government work, he had to resort to written tests. The proportion of first sections in the final examination, which was difficult, was so large that Carl was sure the reader must have marked too leniently, and looked over the papers himself. His results were the same as the reader's, and, he felt, could justifiably be used as some proof of his theory that, if a student is interested in the subject, you cannot keep him from doing good work.

I quote here from two letters written by Washington students who had been under his influence but five months.

"May I, as only a student, add my inadequate sympathy for the loss of Dr. Parker — the most liberal man I have known. While his going from my educative life can be nothing as compared to his loss from a very beautiful family group, yet the enthusiasm, the radiance of his personality — freely given in his classes during the semester I was privileged to know him — made possible to me a greater realization of the fascination of humanity than I obtained during my previous four years of college study. I still look for him to enter the classroom, nor shall I soon forget his ideals, his faith in humanity." From the second letter: "To have known Mr. Parker as well as I did makes me feel that I was indeed privileged, and I shall

always carry with me the charm and inspiration of
his glorious personality. The campus was never so
sad as on the day which brought the news of his
death — it seemed almost incredible that one man in
five short months could have left so indelible an
impress of his character on the student body."

Besides being of real influence on the campus, he
had the respect and confidence of the business world,
both labor and capital; and in addition, he stood as
the representative of the Government in labor-adjust-
ments and disputes. And — it was of lesser conse-
quence, but oh it *did* matter — *we had money enough
to live on!!* We had made ourselves honestly think
that we had just about everything we wanted on
what we got, plus outside lectures, in California. But
once we had tasted of the new-found freedom of truly
enough; once there was gone forever the stirring
around to pick up a few extra dollars here and there
to make both ends meet; once we knew for the first
time the satisfaction and added joy that come from
some responsible person to help with the housework
— we felt that we were soaring through life with our
feet hardly touching the ground.

Instead of my spending most of the day in the
kitchen and riding herd on the young, we had our
dropped-straight-from-heaven Mrs. Willard. And see
what that meant. Every morning at nine I left the
house with Carl, and we walked together to the
University. As I think of those daily walks now, arm-
in-arm, rain or shine, I'd not give up the memory of
them for all creation. Carl would go over what he

was to talk about that morning in Introductory Economics (how it would have raised the hair of the orthodox Econ.I teacher!), and of course we always
talked some of what marvelous children we possessed.
Carl would begin: "Tell me some more about the
June-Bug!"

He would go to his nine o'clock, I to mine. After
my ten-o'clock class, and on the way to my eleven-
o'clock lecture, I always ran in to his office a second,
to gossip over what mail he had got that morning
and how things were going generally. Then, at twelve,
in his office again. "Look at this telegram that just
came in." "How shall I answer Mr. ——'s about that
job?" And then home together; not once a week, but
every day.

Afternoons, except the three afternoons when I
played hockey, I was at home; but always there was
a possibility that Carl would ring up about five. "I
am at a meeting down-town. Can't get things settled,
so we continue this evening. Run down and have supper with me, and perhaps, who knows, a Bill Hart
film might be around town!" There was Mrs. Willard
who knew just what to do, and off I could fly to see
my husband. You can't, on $1700 a year.

I hear people nowadays scold and roar over the
pay the working classes are getting, and how they
are spending it all on nonsense and not saving a cent.
I stand it as long as I can and then I burst out. For
I, too, have tasted the joy of at last being able to get
things we never thought we would own and of feeling
the wings of financial freedom feather out where, be-

fore, all had been cold calculation: Can we do this? if so, what must we give up? I wish every one on earth could feel it. I do not care if they do not save a cent.

Only I do wish my Carl could have experienced those joys a little longer. It was so good — so good, while it lasted! And it was only just starting. Every new call he got to another university was at a salary from one to two thousand dollars more than what we were getting, even at Seattle. It looked as if our days of financial scrimping were gone forever. We even discussed a Ford! nay — even a four-cylinder Buick! And every other Sunday we had fricasseed chicken, and always, always a frosting on the cake. For the first two months in Seattle we felt as if we ought to have company at every meal. It did not seem right to sit down to food as good as that, with just the family present. And it was such fun to bring home unexpected guests, and to know that Mrs. Willard could concoct a dream of a dish while the guests were removing their hats; and I not having to miss any of the conversation from being in the kitchen. Every other Sunday night we had the whole Department and their wives to Sunday supper — sixteen of them. Oh dear, oh dear, money does make a difference. We grew more determined than ever to see that more folk in the world got more of it.

And yet, in a sense, Carl was a typical professor in his unconcern over matters financial. He started in the first month we were married by turning over every cent to me as a matter of course; and from the beginning of each month to the end, he never had the remotest idea how much money we possessed or what it was spent for. So far as his peace of mind went, on the whole, he was a capitalist. He knew we needed more money than he was making at the University of California, therefore he made all he could on the outside, and came home and dumped it in my lap. From one year's end to the next, he spent hardly five cents on himself — a new suit now and then, a new hat, new shirts at a sale, but never a penny that was not essential.

On the rest of us — there he needed a curbing hand! I discovered him negotiating to buy me a set of jade when he was getting one hundred dollars a month. He would bring home a box of peaches or a tray of berries, when they were first in the market and eaten only by bank presidents and railway magnates, and beam and say, "Guess what surprise I have for you!" Nothing hurt his feelings more than to have him suggest I should buy something for myself, and have me answer that we could not afford it. "Then I'll dig sewers on the side!" he would exclaim. "You buy it, and I'll find the money for it somewhere." If he had turned off at an angle of fifty degrees when he first started his earthly career, he would have been a star example of the individual who presses the palms of his hands together and murmurs, "The Lord will provide!"

I never knew a man who was so far removed from the traditional ideas of the proper position of the male head of a household. He felt, as I have said, that he was not the one to have control over finances — that was the wife's province. Then he had another attitude which certainly did not jibe with the Lord-of-the-Manor idea. Perhaps there would be something I wanted to do, and I would wait to ask him about it when he got home. Invariably the same thing would happen. He would take my two hands and put them so that I held his coat-lapels. Then he would place his hands on my shoulders, beam all over, eyes twinkling, and say: —

"Who's boss of this household, anyway?"

And I *had* to answer, "I am."

"Who gets her own way one hundred per cent?"

"I do."

"Who never gets his own way and never wants to get his own way?"

"You."

"Well, then, you know perfectly well you are to do anything in this world you want to do." With a chuckle he would add, "Think of it — not a look-in in my own home!"

Seattle, as I look back on it, meant the unexpected — in every way. Our little sprees together were not the planned-out ones of former years. From the day Carl left Castle Crags, his time was never his own; we could never count on anything from one day to the next — a strike here, an arbitration there, government orders for this, some investigation needed for that. It was harassing, it was wearying. But always every few days there would be that telephone ring which I grew both to dread and to love. For as often as it said, "I've got to go to Tacoma," it also said, "You Girl, put on your hat and coat this minute and come down town while I have a few minutes off — we'll have supper together anyhow."

And the feeling of the courting days never left us — that almost sharp joy of being together again when we just locked arms for a block and said almost nothing — nothing to repeat. And the good-bye that always meant a wrench, always, though it might mean being together within a few hours. And always the waving from the one on the back of the car to the one standing on the corner. Nothing, nothing, ever got tame. After ten years, if Carl ever found himself a little early to catch the train for Tacoma, say, though he had said good-bye but a half an hour before and was to be back that evening, he would find a telephone-booth and ring up to say, perhaps, that he was glad he had married me! Mrs. Willard once said that after hearing Carl or me talk to the other over the telephone, it made other husbands and wives when they telephoned sound as if they must be contemplating divorce. But telephoning was an event: it was a little extra present from Providence, as it were.

And I think of two times when we met accidentally on the street in Seattle — it seemed something we could hardly believe: all the world — the war, commerce, industry — stopped while we tried to realize what had happened.

Then, every night that he had to be out, — and he had to be out night after night in Seattle, — I would hear his footstep coming down the street; it would wake me, though he wore rubber heels. He would fix the catch on the front-door lock, then come upstairs, calling out softly, "You awake?" He always knew I was. Then, sitting on the edge of the bed, he would tell all the happenings since I had seen him last. Once in a while he'd sigh and say, "A little ranch up on the Clearwater would go pretty well about now, would n't it, my girl?" And I would sigh, and say, "Oh dear, would n't it?"

I remember once, when we were first married, he got home one afternoon before I did. When I opened the door to our little Seattle apartment, there he was, walking the floor, looking as if the bottom had dropped out of the universe. "I've had the most awful twenty minutes," he informed me, "simply terrible. Promise me absolutely that never, never will you let me get home before you do. To expect to find you home and then open the door into empty rooms — oh, I never lived through such a twenty minutes!" We had a lark's whistle that we had used since before our engaged days. Carl would whistle it under my window at the Theta house in college, and I would run down and out the side door, to the utter disgust of my well-bred "sisters," who arranged to make cutting remarks at the table about it in the hope that I would reform my "servant-girl tactics." That whistle was whistled through those early Seattle days, through Oakland, through Cambridge, Leipzig, Berlin, Heidelberg, Munich, Swanage, Berkeley, Alamo in the country, Berkeley again (he would start it way down the hill so I could surely hear), Castle Crags, and Seattle. Wherever any of us were in the house, it meant a dash for all to the front door — to welcome the Dad home.

One evening I was scanning some article on marriage by the fire in Seattle — it was one of those rare times that Carl too was at home and going over lectures for the next day. It held that, to be successful, marriage had to be an adjustment — a giving in here by the man, there by the woman.

I said to Carl: "If that is true, you must have been doing all the adjusting; I never have had to give up, or fit in, or relinquish one little thing, so you've been doing it all."

He thought for a moment, then answered: "You know, I've heard that too, and wondered about it. For I know I've given up nothing, made no 'adjustments.' On the contrary, I seem always to have been getting more than a human being had any right to count on."

It was that way, even to the merest details, such as both liking identically the same things to eat, seasoned the identical way. We both liked to do the identical things, without a single exception. Perhaps one exception — he had a fondness in his heart for firearms that I could not share. (The gleam in his eyes when he got out his collection every so often to clean and oil it!) I liked guns, provided I did not have to shoot at anything alive with them; but pistols I just plain did not like at all. We rarely could pass one of these shooting-galleries without trying our luck at five cents for so many turns — at clay pigeons or rabbits whirling around on whatnots; but that was as wild as I ever wanted to get with a gun.

We liked the same friends without exception, the same books, the same pictures, the same music. He wrote once: "We (the two of us) love each other, like to do things together (absolutely anything), don't need or want anybody else, and the world is ours." Mrs. Willard once told me that if she had read about our life together in a book, she would not have believed it. She did not know that any one on earth could live like that. Perhaps that is one reason why I want to tell about it — because it was just so plain wonderful day in, day out. I feel, too, that I have a complete record of our life. For fourteen years, every day that we were not together we wrote to each other, with the exception of two short camping-trips that Carl made, where mail could be sent out only by chance returning campers.

Somehow I find myself thinking here of our wedding anniversaries, — spread over half the globe, — and the joy we got out of just those ten occasions. The first one was back in Oakland, after our return from Seattle. We still had elements of convention left in us then, — or, rather, I still had some; I don't believe Carl had a streak of it in him ever, — so we dressed in our very best clothes, dress-suit and all, and had dinner at the Key Route Inn, where we had gone after the wedding a year before. After dinner we rushed home, I nursed the son, we changed into natural clothes, and went to the circus. I had misgivings

about the circus being a fitting wedding-anniversary
celebration; but what was one to do when the circus
comes to town but one night in the year?

The second anniversary was in Cambridge. We always used to laugh each year and say: "Gracious!
if any one had told us a year ago we'd be here this
September seventh!" Every year we were somewhere
we never dreamed we would be. That first September
seventh, the night of the wedding, we were to be in
Seattle for years — selling bonds. What a fearful
prospect in retrospect, compared to what we really
did! The second September, back in Oakland, we
thought we were to be in the bond business for years
in Oakland. More horrible thoughts as I look back
upon it. The third September seventh, the second
anniversary, lo and behold, was in Cambridge, Massachusetts! Whoever would have guessed it, in all the
world? It was three days after Carl's return from
that awful Freiburg summer — we left Nandy with
a kind-hearted neighbor, and away we spreed to Boston, to the matinée and something good to eat.

Then, whoever would have imagined for a moment
that the next year we would be celebrating in Berlin
— dinner at the Café Rheingold, with wine! The
fourth anniversary was at Heidelberg — one of the
red-letter days, as I look back upon those magic
years. We left home early, with our lunch, which we
ate on a bed of dry leaves in a fairy birch forest back
— and a good ways up — in the Odenwald. Then
we walked and walked — almost twenty-five miles
all told — through little forest hamlets, stopping now

and then at some small inn along the roadside for a
cheese sandwich or a glass of beer. By nightfall we
reached Neckarsteinach and the railroad, and prowled
around the twisted narrow streets till train-time, gazing often at our beloved Dilsberg crowning the hilltop
across the river, her ancient castle tower and town
walls showing black against the starlight. The happiness, the foreign untouristed wonder of that day!

Our fifth anniversary was another red-letter day —
one of the days that always made me feel, in looking
back on it, that we must have been people in a novel,
an English novel; that it could not really have been
Carl and I who walked that perfect Saturday from
Swanage to Studland. But it was our own two joyous
souls who explored that quaint English thatched-roof,
moss-covered corner of creation; who poked about
the wee old mouldy church and cemetery; who had
tea and muffins and jam out under an old gnarled
apple tree behind a thatched-roof cottage. What a
wonder of a day it was! And indeed it was my Carl
and I who walked the few miles home toward sunset,
swinging hands along the downs, and fairly speechless
with the glory of five years married and England
and our love. I should like to be thinking of that day
just before I die. It was so utterly perfect, and so
ours.

Our sixth anniversary was another, yes, yet another
red-letter memory — one of those times that the
world seemed to have been leading up to since it first
cooled down. We left our robust sons in the care of
our beloved aunt, Elsie Turner, — this was back in

Berkeley, — and one Saturday we fared forth, plus sleeping-bags, frying-pan, fishing-rod, and a rifle. We rode to the end of the Ocean Shore Line — but first got off the train at Half Moon Bay, bought half a dozen eggs from a lonely-looking female, made for the beach, and fried said eggs for supper. Then we got back on another train, and stepped off at the end of the line, in utter darkness. We decided that somewhere we should find a suitable wooded nook where we could sequester ourselves for the night. We stumbled along until we could not see another inch in front of us for the dark and the thick fog; so made camp — which meant spreading out two bags — in what looked like as auspicious a spot as was findable. When we opened our eyes to the morning sunlight, we discovered we were on a perfectly barren open ploughed piece of land, and had slept so near the road that if a machine passing along in the night had skidded out a bit to the side, it would have removed our feet.

That day, Sunday, was our anniversary, and the Lord was with us early and late, though not obtrusively. We got a farmer out of bed to buy some eggs for our breakfast. He wanted to know what we were doing out so early, anyhow. We told him, celebrating our sixth wedding anniversary. Whereat he positively refused to take a cent for the eggs — wedding present, he said. Around noon we passed a hunter, who stopped to chat, and ended by presenting us with a cotton-tail rabbit to cook for dinner. And such a dinner! — by a bit of a stream up in the hills. That afternoon, late, we stumbled on a deserted farmhouse almost at the summit — trees laden with apples and the ground red with them, pears and a few peaches for the picking, and a spring of ice-cold water with one lost fat trout in it that I tried for hours to catch by fair means or foul; but he merely waved his tail slowly, as if to say, "One wedding present you don't get!" We slept that night on some hay left in an old barn — lots of mice and gnawy things about; but I could not get nearly as angry at a gnawy mouse as at a fat conceited trout who refused to be caught.

Next day was a holiday, so we kept on our way rejoicing, and slept that night under great redwoods, beside a stream where trout had better manners. After a fish breakfast we potted a tin can full of holes with the rifle, and then bore down circuitously and regretfully on Redwood City and the Southern Pacific Railway, and home and college and dishes to wash and socks to darn — but uproarious and joyful sons to compensate.

The seventh anniversary was less exciting, but that could not be helped. We were over in Alamo, with my father, small brother, and sister visiting us at the time — or rather, of course, the place was theirs to begin with. There was no one to leave the blessed sons with; also, Carl was working for the Immigration and Housing Commission, and no holidays. But he managed to get home a bit early; we had an early supper, got the sons in bed, hitched up the old horse to the old cart, and off we fared in the moonlight, married seven years and not sorry. We just poked about, ending at Danville with Danville ice-cream and Danville pumpkin pie; then walked the horse all the way back to Alamo and home.

Our eighth anniversary, as mentioned, was in our very own home in Berkeley, with the curtains drawn, the telephone plugged, and our Europe spread out before our eyes.

The ninth anniversary was still too soon after the June-Bug's arrival for me to get off the hill and back, up our two hundred and seventeen steps home, so we celebrated under our own roof again — this time with a roast chicken and ice-cream dinner, and with the entire family participating — except the June-Bug, who did almost nothing then but sleep. I tell you, if ever we had chicken, the bones were not worth salvaging by the time we got through. We made it last at least two meals, and a starving tom cat would pass by what was left with a scornful sniff.

Our tenth and last anniversary was in Seattle. Carl had to be at Camp Lewis all day, but he got back in time to meet me at six-thirty in the lobby of the Hotel Washington. From there we went to our own favorite place — Blanc's — for dinner. Shut away behind a green lattice arbor-effect, we celebrated ten years of joy and riches and deep contentment, and as usual asked ourselves, "What in the world shall we be doing a year from now? Where in the world shall we be?" And as usual we answered, "Bring the future what it may, we have *ten years* that no power in heaven or earth can rob us of!"

There was another occasion in our lives that I want

to put down in black and white, though it does not come under wedding anniversaries. But it was such a celebration! "Uncle Max" 'lowed that before we left Berkeley we must go off on a spree with him, and suggested — imagine! — Del Monte! The twelve-and-a-half-cent Parkers at Del Monte! That was one spot we had never seen ourselves even riding by. We got our beloved Nurse Balch out to stay with the young, and when a brand-new green Pierce Arrow, about the size of our whole living-room, honked without, we were ready, bag and baggage, for a spree such as we had never imagined ourselves having in this world or the next. We called for the daughter of the head of the Philosophy Department. Max had said to bring a friend along to make four; so, four, we whisked the dust of Berkeley from our wheels and — presto — Del Monte!

Parents of three children, who do most of their own work besides, do not need to be told in detail what those four days meant. Parents of three children know what the hours of, say, seven to nine mean, at home; nor does work stop at nine. It is one mad whirl to get the family ears washed and teeth cleaned, and "Chew your mush!" and "Wipe your mouth!" and "Where's your speller?" and "Jim, come back here and put on your rubbers!" ("Where are my rubbers?" Ach Gott! where?) Try six times to get the butcher — line busy. Breakfast dishes to clear up; baby to bathe, dress, feed. Count the laundry. Forget all about the butcher until fifteen minutes before dinner. Laundry calls. Telephone rings seven times. Neighbor calls to borrow an egg. Telephone the milkman for a pound of butter. Make the beds, — telephone rings in the middle, — two beds do not get made till three. Start lunch. Wash the baby's clothes. Telephone rings three times while you are in the basement. Rice burns. Door-bell — gas and electric bill. Telephone rings. Patch boys' overalls. Water-bill. Stir the pudding. Telephone rings. Try to read at least the table of contents of the "New Republic." Neighbor calls to return some flour. Stir the pudding again. Mad stamping up the front steps. Sons home. Forget to scrape their feet. Forget to take off their rubbers. Dad's whistle. Hurray! Lunch.— Let's stop about here, and return to Del Monte.

This is where music would help. The Home *motif* would be — I do not know those musical terms, but a lot of jumpy notes up and down the piano, fast and never catching up. Del Monte *motif* slow, lazy melody — ending with dance-music for night-time. In plain English, what Del Monte meant was a care-free, absolutely care-free, jaunt into another world. It was not our world, — we could have been happy forever did we never lay eyes on Del Monte, — and yet, oh, it was such fun! Think of lazing in bed till eight or eight-thirty, then taking a leisurely bath, then dressing and deliberately using up time doing it — put one shoe on and look at it a spell; then, when you are good and ready, put on the next. Just feeling sort of spunky about it — just wanting to show some one that time is nothing to you — what's the hurry?

Then — oh, what *motif* in music could do a Del

Monte breakfast justice? Just yesterday you were gulping down a bite, in between getting the family fed and off. Here you were, holding hands under the table to make sure you were not dreaming, while you took minutes and minutes to eat fruit and mush and eggs and coffee and waffles, and groaned to think there was still so much on the menu that would cost you nothing to keep on consuming, but where, oh, where, put it? After rocking a spell in the sun on the front porch, the green Pierce Arrow appears, and all honk off for the day — four boxes of picnic lunch stowed away by a gracious waiter; not a piece of bread for it did you have to spread yourself. Basking in the sun under cypress trees, talking over every subject under heaven; back in time for a swim, a rest before dinner; then dinner (why, oh, why has the human such biological limitations?). Then a concert, then dancing, then — crowning glory of an unlimited bank-account — Napa soda lemonade — and bed. Oh, what a four days!

In thinking over the intimate things of our life together, I have difficulty in deciding what the finest features of it were. There was so much that made it rich, so much to make me realize I was blessed beyond any one else, that I am indebted to the world forever for the color that living with Carl Parker gave to existence. Perhaps one of the most helpful memories to me now is the thought of his absolute faith in me. From the time we were first in love, it meant a new zest in life to know that Carl firmly believed there was nothing I could not do. For all that I hold no orthodox belief in immortality, I could no more get away from the idea that, if I fail in anything now — why I *can't* fail — think of Carl's faith in me! About four days before he died, he looked up at me once as I was arranging his pillow and said, so seriously, "You know, there is n't a university in the country that would n't give you your Ph.D. without your taking an examination for it." He was delirious, it is true; but nevertheless it expressed, though indeed in a very exaggerated form, the way he had of thinking I was somebody! I knew there was no one in the world like him, but I had sound reasons for that. Oh, but it is wonderful to live with some one who thinks you are wonderful! It does not make you conceited, not a bit, but it makes a happy singing feeling in your heart to feel that the one you love best in the world is proud of you. And there is always the incentive of vowing that some day you will justify it all.

The fun of dressing for a party in a hand-me-down dress from some relative, knowing that the one you want most to please will honestly believe, and say on the way home, that you were the best-looking one at the party! The fun of cooking for a man who thinks every dish set before him is the best food he *ever* ate — and not only say it, but act that way. ("That was just a sample. Give me a real dish of it, now that I know it's the best pudding I ever tasted!")

CHAPTER XVI

As soon as the I.W.W. article was done, Carl had to begin on his paper to be read before the Economic Association, just after Christmas, in Philadelphia. That was fun working over. "Come up here and let me read you this!" And we'd go over that much of the paper together. Then more reading to Miss Van Doren, more correctings, finally finishing it just the day before he had to leave. But that was partly because he had to leave earlier than expected. The Government had telegraphed him to go on to Washington, to mediate a threatened longshoremen's strike. Carl worked harder over the longshoremen than over any other single labor difficulty, not excepting the eight-hour day in lumber. Here again I do not feel free to go into details. The matter was finally, at Carl's suggestion, taken to Washington.

The longshoremen interested Carl for the same reason that the migratory and the I.W.W. interested him; in fact, there were many I.W.W. among them. It was the lower stratum of the labor-world — hard physical labor, irregular work, and, on the whole, undignified treatment by the men set over them. And they reacted as Carl expected men in such a position to react. Yet, on the side of the workers, he felt that in this particular instance it was a case of men being led by stubborn egotistical union delegates not really representing the wishes of the rank and file of union members, their main idea being to compromise on nothing. On the other hand, be it said that he considered the employers he had to deal with here the fairest, most open-minded, most anxious to compromise in the name of justice, of all the groups of employers he ever had to deal with. The whole affair was nerve-racking, as is best illustrated by the fact that, while Carl was able to hold the peace as long as he was on the job, three days after his death the situation "blew up."

On his way East he stopped off in Spokane, to talk with the lumbermen east of the mountains. There, at a big meeting, he was able to put over the eight-hour day. The Wilson Mediation Commission was in Seattle at the time. Felix Frankfurter telephoned out his congratulations to me, and said: "We consider it the single greatest achievement of its kind since the United States entered the war." The papers were full of it and excitement ran high. President Wilson was telegraphed to by the Labor Commission, and he in turn telegraphed back his pleasure. In addition, the East Coast lumbermen agreed to Carl's scheme of an employment manager for their industry, and detailed him to find a man for the job while in the East. My, but I was excited!

Not only that, but they bade fair to let him inaugurate a system which would come nearer than any chance he could have expected to try out on a big scale his theories on the proper handling of labor. The men were to have the sanest recreation devisable for their needs and interests — out-of-door sports, movies, housing that would permit of dignified family life, recreation centres, good and proper food, alteration in the old order of "hire and fire," and general control over the men. Most employers argued: "Don't forget that the type of men we have in the lumber camps won't know how to make use of a single reform you suggest, and probably won't give a straw for the whole thing." To which Carl would reply: "Don't forget that your old conditions have drawn the type of man you have. This won't change men over-night by a long shot, but it will at once relieve the tension — and see, in five years, if your type itself has not undergone a change."

From Washington, D.C., he wrote: "This city is one mad mess of men, desolate, and hunting for folks they should see, overcharged by hotels, and away from their wives." The red-letter event of Washington was when he was taken for tea to Justice Brandeis's. "We talked I.W.W., unemployment, etc., and he was oh, so grand!" A few days later, two days before Christmas, Mrs. Brandeis telephoned and asked him for Christmas dinner! That was a great event in the Parker annals — Justice Brandeis having been a hero among us for some years. Carl wrote: "He is all he is supposed to be and more." He in turn wrote me after Carl's death: "Our country shares with you the great loss. Your husband was among the very few Americans who possessed the character, knowledge, and insight which are indispensable in dealing effectively with our labor-problem. Appreciation of his value was coming rapidly, and

events were enforcing his teachings. His journey to
the East brought inspiration to many; and I seek
comfort in the thought that, among the students at
the University, there will be some at least who are
eager to carry forward his work."

There were sessions with Gompers, Meyer Bloom-
field, Secretary Baker, Secretary Daniels, the Ship-
ping Board, and many others.

Then, at Philadelphia, came the most telling single
event of our economic lives — Carl's paper before
the Economic Association on "Motives in Economic
Life." At the risk of repeating to some extent the
ideas quoted from previous papers, I shall record here
a few statements from this one, as it gives the last
views he held on his field of work.

"Our conventional economics to-day analyzes no
phase of industrialism or the wage-relationship, or
citizenship in pecuniary society, in a manner to offer
a key to such distressing and complex problems as
this. Human nature riots to-day through our economic
structure, with ridicule and destruction; and we economists look on helpless and aghast. The menace of the
war does not seem potent to quiet revolt or still class
cries. The anxiety and apprehension of the economist
should not be produced by this cracking of his economic system, but by the poverty of the criticism of
industrialism which his science offers. Why are
economists mute in the presence of a most obvious
crisis in our industrial society? Why have our criticisms of industrialism no sturdy warnings about this
unhappy evolution? Why does an agitated officialdom

search to-day in vain among our writings, for scientific advice touching labor-inefficiency or industrial disloyalty, for prophecies and plans about the rise in our industrialism of economic classes unharmonious and hostile?

"The fair answer seems this: We economists speculate little on human motives. We are not curious about the great basis of fact which dynamic and behavioristic psychology has gathered to illustrate the instinct stimulus to human activity. Most of us are not interested to think of what a psychologically full or satisfying life is. We are not curious to know that a great school of behavior analysis called the Freudian has been built around the analysis of the energy outbursts brought by society's balking of the native human instincts. Our economic literature shows that we are but rarely curious to know whether industrialism is suited to man's inherited nature, or what man in turn will do to our rules of economic conduct in case these rules are repressive. The motives to economic activity which have done the major service in orthodox economic texts and teachings have been either the vague middle-class virtues of thrift, justice, and solvency, or the equally vague moral sentiments of 'striving for the welfare of others,' 'desire for the larger self,' 'desire to equip one's self well,' or, lastly, the labor-saving deduction that man is stimulated in all things economic by his desire to satisfy his wants with the smallest possible effort. All this gentle parody in motive theorizing continued contemporaneously with the output of the rich literature of social and behavioristic psychology which was almost entirely addressed to this very problem of human motives in modern economic society. Noteworthy exceptions are the remarkable series of books by Veblen, the articles and criticisms of Mitchell and Patten, and the most significant small book by Taussig, entitled 'Inventors and Money-makers.' It is this complementary field of psychology to which the economists must turn, as these writers have turned, for a vitalization of their basic hypotheses. There awaits them a bewildering array of studies of the motives, emotions, and folk-ways of our pecuniary civilization. Generalizations and experiment statistics abound, ready-made for any structure of economic criticism. The human motives are isolated, described, compared. Business confidence, the release of work-energy, advertising appeal, market vagaries, the basis of value computations, decay of workmanship, the labor unrest, decline in the thrift habit, are the subjects treated.

"All human activity is untiringly actuated by the demand for realization of the instinct wants. If an artificially limited field of human endeavor be called economic life, all its so-called motives hark directly back to the human instincts for their origin. *There are, in truth, no economic motives as such.* The motives of economic life are the same as those of the life of art, of vanity and ostentation, of war and crime, of sex. Economic life is merely the life in which instinct gratification is alleged to take on a rational pecuniary habit form. Man is not less a father, with a father's parental instinct, just because he passes down the

street from his home to his office. His business raid
into his rival's market has the same naïve charm
that tickled the heart of his remote ancestor when in
the night he rushed the herds of a near-by clan. A
manufacturer tries to tell a conventional world that
he resists the closed shop because it is un-American,
it loses him money, or it is inefficient. A few years
ago he was more honest, when he said he would run
his business as he wished and would allow no man
to tell him what to do. His instinct of leadership, re-
inforced powerfully by his innate instinctive revulsion to the confinement of the closed shop, gave the
true stimulus. His opposition is psychological, not
ethical."

He then goes on to catalogue and explain the following instincts which he considered of basic importance in any study of economics: (1) gregariousness;
(2) parental bent, motherly behavior, kindliness;
(3) curiosity, manipulation, workmanship; (4) acqui-
sition, collecting, ownership; (5) fear and flight;
(6) mental activity, thought; (7) the housing or set-
tling instinct; (8) migration, homing; (9) hunting
("Historic revivals of hunting urge make an interesting recital of religious inquisitions, witch-burnings,
college hazings, persecution of suffragettes, of the
I.W.W., of the Japanese, or of pacifists. All this goes
on often under naïve rationalization about justice and
patriotism, but it is pure and innate lust to run something down and hurt it"); (10) anger, pugnacity;
(11) revolt at confinement, at being limited in liberty
of action and choice; (12) revulsion; (13) leadership

and mastery; (14) subordination, submission; (15) display, vanity, ostentation; (16) sex.

After quoting from Professor Cannon, and discussing the contributions that his studies have made to the subject of man's reaction to his immediate environment, he continues: —

"The conclusion seems both scientific and logical, that behavior in anger, fear, pain, and hunger is a basically different behavior from behavior under repose and economic security. The emotions generated under the conditions of existence-peril seem to make the emotions and motives generative in quiet and peace pale and unequal. It seems impossible to avoid the conclusion that the most vital part of man's inheritance is one which destines him to continue for some myriads of years ever a fighting animal when certain conditions exist in his environment. Though, through education, man be habituated in social and intelligent behavior or, through license, in sexual debauchery, still, at those times when his life or liberty is threatened, his instinct-emotional nature will inhibit either social thought or sex ideas, and present him as merely an irrational fighting animal. . . .

"The instincts and their emotions, coupled with the obedient body, lay down in scientific and exact description the motives which must and will determine human conduct. If a physical environment set itself against the expression of these instinct motives, the human organism is fully and efficiently prepared for a tenacious and destructive revolt against this environment; and if the antagonism persist, the organ-

ism is ready to destroy itself and disappear as a species
if it fail of a psychical mutation which would make
the perverted order endurable."

And in conclusion, he states: —

"The dynamic psychology of to-day describes the
present civilization as a repressive environment. For
a great number of its inhabitants a sufficient self-
expression is denied. There is, for those who care to
see, a deep and growing unrest and pessimism. With
the increase in knowledge is coming a new realization
of the irrational direction of economic evolution. The
economists, however, view economic inequality and
life-degradation as objects in truth outside the science.
Our value-concept is a price-mechanism hiding behind a phrase. If we are to play a part in the social
readjustment immediately ahead, we must put human
nature and human motives into our basic hypotheses.
Our value-concept must be the yardstick to measure
just how fully things and institutions contribute to a
full psychological life. We must know more of the
meaning of progress. The domination of society by one
economic class has for its chief evil the thwarting of
the instinct life of the subordinate class and the perversion of the upper class. The extent and characteristics of this evil are to be estimated only when we
know the innate potentialities and inherited propensi-
ties of man; and the ordering of this knowledge and
its application to the changeable economic structure
is the task before the trained economist to-day."

A little later I saw one of the big men who was at
that Economic Association meeting, and he said: "I

don't see why Parker is n't spoiled. He was the most talked-about man at the Convention." Six publishing houses wrote, after that paper, to see if he could enlarge it into a book. Somehow it did seem as if now more than ever the world was ours. We looked ahead into the future, and wondered if it could seem as good to any one as it did to us. It was almost *too* good — we were dazed a bit by it. It is one of the things I just cannot let myself ever think of — that future and the plans we had. Anything I can ever do now would still leave life so utterly dull by comparison.

CHAPTER XVII

ONE of the days in Seattle that I think of most was about a month before the end. The father of a great friend of ours died, and Carl and I went to the funeral one Sunday afternoon. We got in late, so stood in a corner by the door, and held hands, and seemed to own each other especially hard that day. Afterwards we prowled around the streets, talking of funerals and old age.

Most of the people there that afternoon were gray-haired — the family had lived in Seattle for years and years, and these were the friends of years and years back. Carl said: "That is something we can't have when you and I die — the old, old friends who have stood by us year in and year out. It is one of the phases of life you sacrifice when you move around at the rate we do. But in the first place, neither of us wants a funeral, and in the second place, we feel that moving gives more than it takes away — so we are satisfied."

Then we talked about our own old age — planned it in detail. Carl declared: "I want you to promise me faithfully you will make me stop teaching when I am sixty. I have seen too much of the tragedy of men hanging on and on and students and education being sacrificed because the teacher has lost his fire — has fallen behind in the parade. I feel now as if I'd never grow old — that does n't mean that I won't. So, no matter how strong I may be going at sixty, make me stop — promise."

Then we discussed our plans: by that time the children would be looking out for themselves, — very much so, — and we could plan as we pleased. It was to be England — some suburb outside of London, where we could get into big things, and yet where we could be peaceful and by ourselves, and read and write, and have the young economists who were traveling about, out to spend week-ends with us; and then we could keep our grandchildren while their parents were traveling in Europe! About a month from that day, he was dead.

There is a path I must take daily to my work at college, which passes through the University Botanical Garden. Every day I must brace myself for it, for there, growing along the path, is a clump of old-fashioned morning glories. Always, from the time we first came back to teach in Berkeley and passed along that same path to the University, we planned to have morning glories like those — the odor came to meet you yards away — growing along the path to the little home we would at last settle down in when we were old. We used always to remark pictures in the newspapers, of So-and-so on their "golden anniversary," and would plan about our own "golden wedding-day" — old age together always seemed so good to think about. There was a time when we used to plan to live in a lighthouse, way out on some point, when we got old. It made a strong appeal, it really

did. We planned many ways of growing old — not
that we talked of it often, perhaps twice a year, but
always, always it was, of course, *together*. Strange,
that neither of us ever dreamed one would grow old
without the other.

And yet, too, there is the other side. I found a letter written during our first summer back in Berkeley,
just after we had said good-bye at the station when
Carl left for Chicago. Among other things he wrote:
"It just makes me feel bad to see other folks living
put-in lives, when we two (four) have loved through
Harvard and Europe and it has only commenced, and
no one is loving so hard or living so happily. . . . I am
most willing to die now (if you die with me), for we
have lived one complete life of joy already." And
then he added — if only the adding of it could have
made it come true: "But we have fifty years yet of
love."

Oh, it was so true that we packed into ten years
the happiness that could normally be considered to
last a lifetime — a long lifetime. Sometimes it seems
almost as if we must have guessed it was to end so
soon, and lived so as to crowd in all the joy we could
while our time together was given us. I say so often
that I stand right now the richest woman in the world
— why talk of sympathy? I have our three precious,
marvelously healthy children, I have perfect health
myself, I have all and more than I can handle of big
ambitious maturing plans, with a chance to see them
carried out, I have enough to live on, and, greatest of
all, fifteen years of perfect memories — And yet, to

hear a snatch of a tune and know that the last time
you heard it you were together — perhaps it was the
very music they played as you left the theatre arm-
in-arm that last night; to put on a dress you have not
worn for some time and remember that, when you
last had it on, it was the night you went, just the two
of you, to Blanc's for dinner; to meet unexpectedly
some friend, and recall that the last time you saw
him it was that night you two, strolling with hands
clasped, met him on Second Avenue accidentally,
and chatted on the corner; to come across a necktie
in a trunk, to read a book he had marked, to see his
handwriting — perhaps just the address on an old
baggage-check — Oh, one can sound so much braver
than one feels! And then, because you have tried so
hard to live up to the pride and faith he had in you,
to be told: "You know I am surprised that you
have n't taken Carl's death harder. You seem to be
just the same exactly."

What is *seeming?* Time and time again, these
months, I have thought, what do any of us know
about what another person *feels?* A smile — a laugh
— I used to think of course they stood for happiness.
There can be many smiles, much laughter, and it
means — nothing. But surely anything is kinder for
a friend to see than tears!

When Carl returned from the East in January, he
was more rushed than ever — his time more filled
than ever with strike mediations, street-car arbitra-
tions, cost of living surveys for the Government, conferences on lumber production. In all, he had mediated

thirty-two strikes, sat on two arbitration boards, made three cost-of-living surveys for the Government. (Mediations did gall him — he grew intellectually impatient over this eternal patching up of what he was wont to call "a rotten system." Of course he saw the war-emergency need of it just then, but what he wanted to work on was, why were mediations ever necessary? what social and economic order would best ensure absence of friction?)

On the campus work piled up. He had promised to give a course on Employment Management, especially to train men to go into the lumber industries with a new vision. (Each big company east of the mountains was to send a representative.) It was also open to seniors in college, and a splendid group it was, almost every one pledged to take up employment management as their vocation on graduation — no fear that they would take it up with a capitalist bias. Then — his friends and I had to laugh, it was so like him — the afternoon of the morning he arrived, he was in the thick of a scrap on the campus over a principle he held to tenaciously — the abolition of the one-year modern-language requirement for students in his college. To use his own expression, he "went to the bat on it," and at a faculty meeting that afternoon it carried. He had been working his little campaign for a couple of months, but in his absence in the East the other side had been busy. He returned just in time for the fray. Every one knows what a farce one year of a modern language is at college; even several of the language teachers themselves were

frank enough to admit it. But it was an academic
tradition! I think the two words that upset Carl most
were "efficiency" and "tradition" — both being used
too often as an excuse for practices that did more
harm than good.

And then came one Tuesday, the fifth of March.
He had his hands full all morning with the continued
threatened upheavals of the longshoremen. About
noon the telephone rang — threatened strike in all
the flour-mills; Dr. Parker must come at once. (I am
reminded of a description which was published of
Carl as a mediator. "He thought of himself as a
physician and of an industry on strike as the patient.
And he did not merely ease the patient's pain with
opiates. He used the knife and tried for permanent
cures.") I finally reached him by telephone; his voice
sounded tired, for he had had a very hard morning.
By one o'clock he was working on the flour-mill situation. He could not get home for dinner. About midnight he appeared, having sat almost twelve hours
steadily on the new flour-difficulty. He was "all in,"
he said.

The next morning, one of the rare instances in our
years together, he claimed that he did not feel like
getting up. But there were four important conferences that day to attend to, besides his work at college. He dressed, ate breakfast, then said he felt fever-
ish. His temperature was 102. I made him get back
into bed — let all the conferences on earth explode.
The next day his temperature was 105. "This has

taught us our lesson — no more living at this pace. I
don't need two reminders that I ought to call a halt."
Thursday, Friday, and Saturday he lay there, too
weary to talk, not able to sleep at all nights; the doctor coming regularly, but unable to tell just what
the trouble was, other than a "breakdown."

Saturday afternoon he felt a little better; we
planned then what we would do when he got well.
The doctor had said that he should allow himself at
least a month before going back to college. One month
given to us! "Just think of the writing I can get done,
being around home with my family!" There was an
article for Taussig half done to appear in the "Quarterly Journal of Economics," a more technical analysis of the I.W.W. than had appeared in the "Atlantic
Monthly"; he had just begun a review for the
"American Journal of Economics" of Hoxie's "Trade-
Unionism." Then he was full of ideas for a second
article he had promised the "Atlantic" — "Is the
United States a Nation?" — "And think of being
able to see all I want of the June-Bug!"

Since he had not slept for three nights, the doctor
left powders which I was to give him for Saturday
night. Still he could not sleep. He thought that, if I
read aloud to him in a monotonous tone of voice, he
could perhaps drop off. I got a high-school copy of
"From Milton to Tennyson," and read every sing-
songy poem I could find — "The Ancient Mariner"
twice, hardly pronouncing the words as I droned
along. Then he began to get delirious.

It is a very terrifying experience — to see for

the first time a person in a delirium, and that person the one you love most on earth. All night long I sat there trying to quiet him — it was always some mediation, some committee of employers he was attending. He would say: "I am so tired — can't you people come to some agreement, so that I can go home and sleep?"

At first I would say: "Dearest, you must be quiet and try to go to sleep." — "But I can't leave the meeting!" He would look at me in such distress. So I learned my part, and at each new discussion he would get into, I would suggest: "Here's Will Ogburn just come — he'll take charge of the meeting for you. You come home with me and go to sleep." So he would introduce Will to the gathering, and add: "Gentlemen, my wife wants me to go home with her and go to sleep — good-bye." For a few moments he would be quiet. Then, "O my Lord, something to investigate! What is it this time?" I would cut in hastily: "The Government feels next week will be plenty of time for this investigation." He would look at me seriously. "Did you ever know the Government to give you a week's time to begin?" Then, "Telegrams — more telegrams! Nobody keeps their word, nobody."

About six o'clock in the morning I could wait no longer and called the doctor. He pronounced it pneumonia — an absolutely different case from any he had ever seen: no sign of it the day before, though it was what he had been watching for all along. Every hospital in town was full. A splendid trained nurse came at once to the house — "the best nurse in the whole city," the doctor announced with relief.

Wednesday afternoon the crisis seemed to have passed. That whole evening he was himself, and I — I was almost delirious from sheer joy. To hear his dear voice again just talking naturally! He noticed the nurse for the first time. He was jovial — happy. "I am going to get some fun out of this now!" he smiled. "And oh, won't we have a time, my girl, while I am convalescing!" And we planned the rosiest weeks any one ever planned. Thursday the nurse shaved him — he not only joked and talked like his dear old self — he looked it as well. (All along he had been cheerful — always told the doctor he was "feeling fine"; never complained of anything. It amused the doctor so one morning, when he was leaning over listening to Carl's heart and lungs, as he lay in more or less of a doze and partial delirium. A twinkle suddenly came into Carl's eye. "You sprung a new necktie on me this morning, did n't you?" Sure enough, it was new.)

Thursday morning the nurse was preparing things for his bath in another room and I was with Carl. The sun was streaming in through the windows and my heart was too contented for words. He said: "Do you know what I've been thinking of so much this morning? I've been thinking of what it must be to go through a terrible illness and not have some one you loved desperately around. I say to myself all the while: 'Just think, my girl was here all the time — my girl will be here all the time!' I've lain here this

morning and wondered more than ever what good
angel was hovering over me the day I met you."

I put this in because it is practically the last thing
he said before delirium came on again, and I love to
think of it. He said really more than that.

In the morning he would start calling for me early
— the nurse would try to soothe him for a while, then
would call me. I wanted to be in his room at night,
but they would not let me — there was an unborn
life to be thought of those days, too. As soon as I
reached his bed, he would clasp my hand and hold it
oh, so tight. "I've been groping for you all night —
all night! Why *don't* they let me find you?" Then, in
a moment, he would not know I was there. Daytimes
I had not left him five minutes, except for my meals.
Several nights they had finally let me be by him, anyway. Saturday morning for the first time since the
crisis the doctor was encouraged. "Things are really
looking up," and "You go out for a few moments in
the sun!"

I walked a few blocks to the Mudgetts' in our department, to tell them the good news, and then back;
but my heart sank to its depths again as soon as I
entered Carl's room. The delirium always affected me
that way: to see the vacant stare in his eyes — no
look of recognition when I entered.

The nurse went out that afternoon. "He's doing
nicely," was the last thing she said. She had not been
gone half an hour — it was just two-fifteen — and I
was lying on her bed watching Carl, when he called,
"Buddie, I'm going — come hold my hand." O my

God — I dashed for him, I clung to him, I told him he could not, must not go — we needed him too terribly, we loved him too much to spare him. I felt so sure of it, that I said: "Why, my love is enough to *keep* you here!"

He would not let me leave him to call the doctor. I just knelt there holding both his hands with all my might, talking, talking, telling him we were not going to let him go. And then, at last, the color came back into his face, he nodded his head a bit, and said, "I'll stay," very quietly. Then I was able to rush for the stairs and tell Mrs. Willard to telephone for the doctor. Three doctors we had that afternoon. They reported the case as "dangerous, but not absolutely hopeless." His heart, which had been so wonderful all along, had given out. That very morning the doctor had said: "I wish my pulse was as strong as that!" and there he lay — no pulse at all. They did everything: our own doctor stayed till about ten, then left, with Carl resting fairly easily. He lived only a block away.

About one-thirty the nurse had me call the doctor again. I could see things were going wrong. Once Carl started to talk rather loud. I tried to quiet him and he said: "Twice I've pulled and fought and struggled to live just for you [one of the times had been during the crisis]. Let me just talk if I want to. I can't make the fight a third time — I'm so tired."

Before the doctor could get there, he was dead.

With our beliefs what they were, there was only one thing to be done. We had never discussed it in detail, but I felt absolutely sure I was doing as he would have me do. His body was cremated, without any service whatsoever — nobody present but one of his brothers and a great friend. The next day the two men scattered his ashes out on the waters of Puget Sound. I feel it was as he would have had it.

"Out of your welded lives — welded in spirit and in the comradeship that you had in his splendid work — you know everything that I could say.

"I grieve for you deeply — and I rejoice for any woman who, for even a few short years, is given the great gift in such a form."

THE END

The Riverside Press

CAMBRIDGE . MASSACHUSETTS

U . S . A